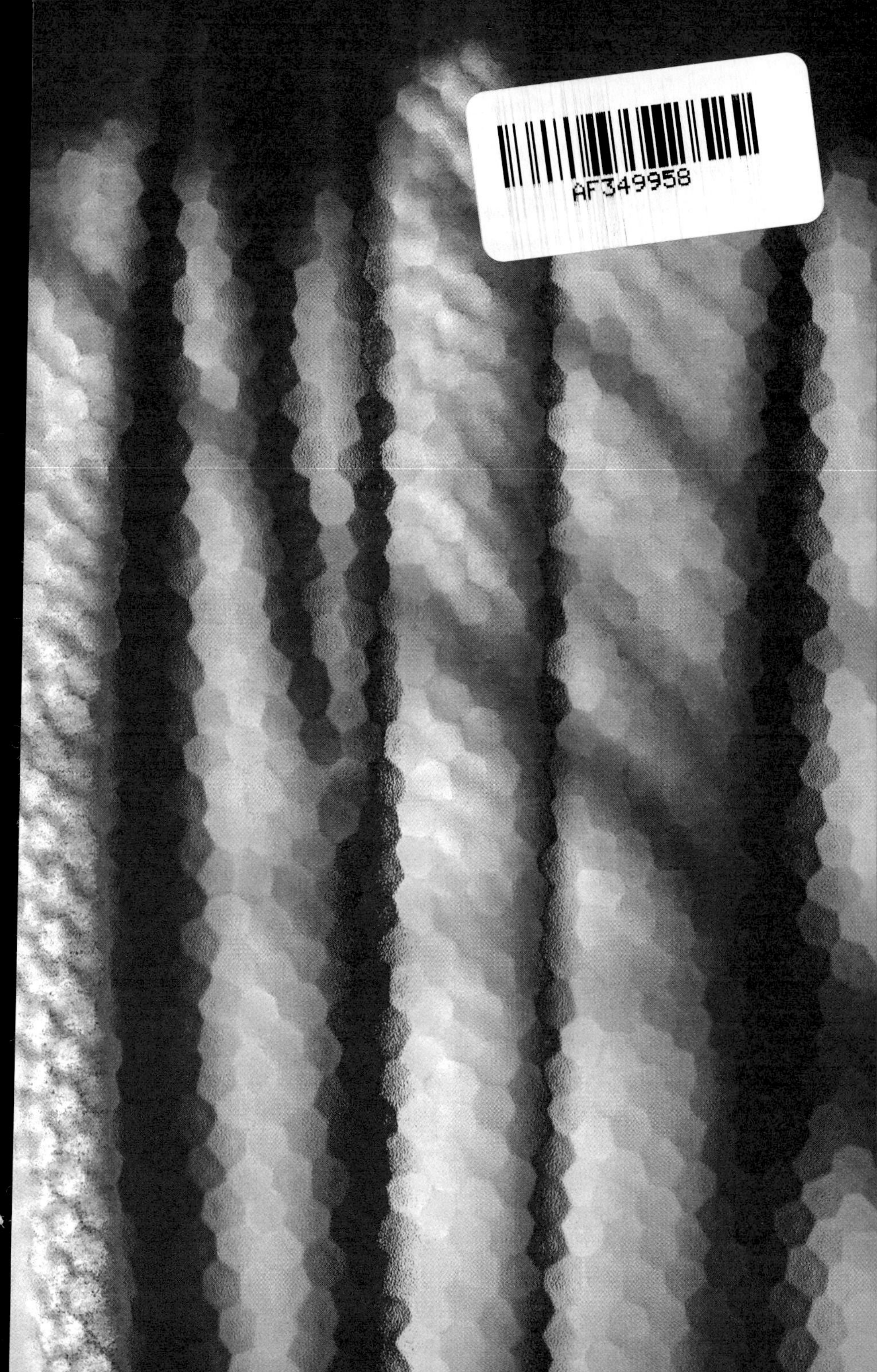
AF349958

In Praise of Shadows and Other Essays

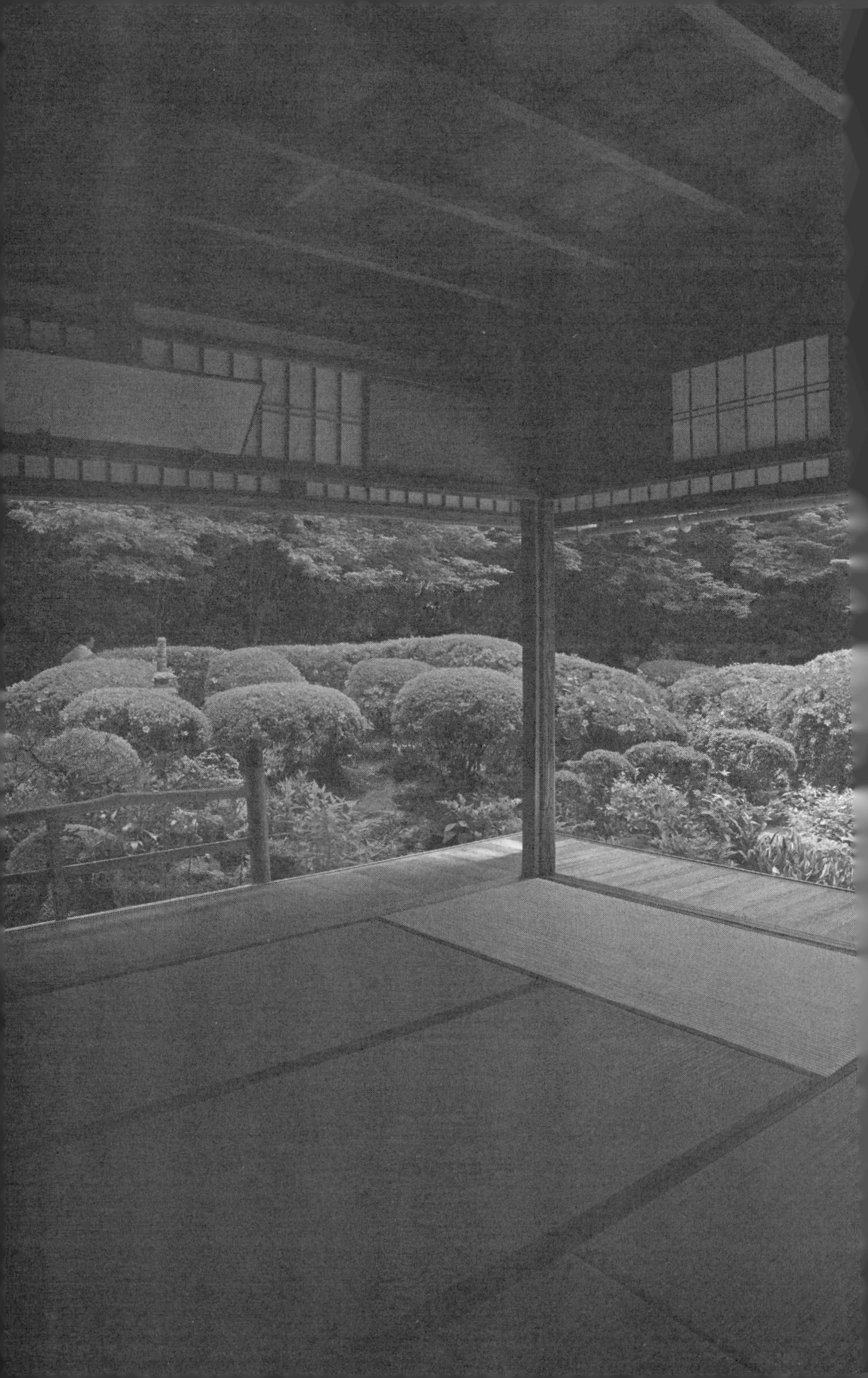

Junichirō Tanizaki

In Praise of Shadows and Other Essays

Translated by **Michael P. Cronin**
Photos by **John Einarsen**

TUTTLE Publishing
Tokyo | Rutland, Vermont | Singapore

Contents

Introduction

Through the Eyes
of an Outsider

By Michael P. Cronin

Tanizaki Junichirō didn't intend to settle down when he moved, in late September of 1923, to the Kansai region, in western Japan, around the cities of Osaka, Kyoto and Kobe. He was fleeing the devastation of the Great Kanto Earthquake of September first, which had destroyed Tokyo and much of the surrounding area, including Tanizaki's home in the nearby port city of Yokohama. The dislocation caused Tanizaki, already a renowned author, considerable culture shock. He moved several times over the next six months, to addresses in Kyoto and in the Hanshin suburbs, between Osaka and Kobe. Eventually, though, he put down roots in Hanshin and ended up living there until his death in 1963. The move became a watershed in his life and career. He would make Kansai the setting for some of his best-loved novels, including *Manji* (*Quicksand*), *Tade kuu mushi* (*Some Prefer Nettles*) and his masterpiece of interwar life, *Sasameyuki* (*The Makioka Sisters*). The move also inspired his best-known work of non-fiction, the essay "In'ei raisan," or "In Praise of Shadows."

A prolific essayist, Tanizaki wrote on a wide variety of subjects, serious and frivolous. His exchange of essays with fellow author Akutagawa Ryūnosuke, conducted in literary journals, over the importance of plot in fiction, constitutes one of the most important literary debates of the modern era. He also wrote several essays on the emerging art of cinema.[1] Nevertheless, his non-fiction writings have drawn relatively little attention outside Japan, in part because few have been available in translation. The exception is "In Praise of Shadows," which has long enjoyed a global readership. Written in 1933, the essay first appeared in English in a heavily abridged translation by Edward Seidensticker (who also translated several of the author's novels), published in the *Japan Quarterly* in 1954 and then republished in the *Atlantic Monthly* the following year. Thomas Harper later expanded this into a complete translation of the essay, published as a book in 1977. A second English translation, by Gregory Starr, appeared in 2017.

The present collection pairs a new translation of "In Praise of Shadows" with three other essays: "Osaka and Osakans as I See Them," written in 1932, and two shorter pieces, "Hanshin Observations" (1925) and "At Okamoto" (1929). These essays overtly concern Tanizaki's relocation; in them, the author details his observations of the culture, society and everyday life of the Kansai region. "In Praise of Shadows," on the other hand, is not overtly *about* the Kansai region but is deeply *informed by* it. Reading these essays together, we better appreciate the significance of the great life-change necessitated by the earthquake and how Tanizaki's growing understanding of, and affection for,

Kansai produced "In Praise of Shadows," an essay that has captured the world's attention.

Tanizaki crossed a great cultural divide in moving from east Japan to west, Kanto to Kansai. Tokyo is, of course, the capital of the modern nation. Even before gaining that status at the time of the Meiji Restoration in 1868, the city was, under its pre-modern name, Edo, the political capital of the Tokugawa Shogunate, which ruled Japan after seizing power in 1603. The cities of Kansai, however, have long boasted their own claims to political and cultural significance. Ancient Kyoto served as Japan's center throughout the Heian period (764–1185), producing a classical golden age, and remained the imperial capital until the Restoration. Cosmopolitan Kobe is an ancient port, home to one of Shinto's oldest shrines, Ikuta Jinja, and the site of the decisive battle in the Genpei War. The area now known as Osaka was the site of Japan's first imperial capital, established in 651; important shrines there have drawn pilgrims for centuries. Osaka became the political capital under the shogun whom Tokugawa Ieyasu betrayed, Toyotomi Hideyoshi, and remained Japan's merchant capital even after political power shifted to the east. Into the modern age, Osaka remained Tokyo's industrial rival—the "smokey capital," "Manchester of the East." A distinct metropolitan culture developed in and around these cities, with its own artistic traditions, vivid dialect and superior cuisine, and inspired a rivalry with the Kanto region.

As an "Edokko," or "child of Edo," born and bred in Tokyo's merchant quarter, Tanizaki reacted predictably, at first, to his relocation—which he seems to have considered a rustication. The earliest of the essays in this collection, "Hanshin Observations," published about two years after the move, certainly betrays his frustration. Eight years later, however, in "Osaka and Osakans as I See Them," he expresses regret for his harsh words and admits to a growing affection for his new home. Nevertheless, he insists, "I shall never lose the essential temperament of a Tokyoite. Therefore, my observations will, to the end, be those made through the eyes of 'a migrant from Tokyo.'" And what did he see through those eyes? Tanizaki closely observes details of speech, dress, personality and customs. At first, he details these with an ethnographic irony shared between himself, as observer, and an implied audience in the capital—and behind the backs, as it were, of the locals—though this gradually changes. ("Hanshin Observations" first appeared in the journal *Bungei shunjū*, published in Tokyo; "At Okamoto" appeared in the *Ōsaka Shinbun* newspaper; and "Osaka and Osakans" was included in a book of essays titled *Ishōan zuihitsu*, using the name he had given to his home in Kobe, "Ishōan," or "hermitage of the leaning pine.") He sees a society unreceptive to a Western-inflected modernity and contrasts it with a Tokyo that is constantly changing under various influences from the West. Furthermore, he sees this unmodernity as an essential quality of the local people, a product of topography, climate and breeding (ignoring the fact that the cities of Kansai, like all modern cities, were full of people from elsewhere). Most important, Tanizaki finds in Osaka traces of the old Tokyo of his childhood—the Tokyo that was already fading before the earthquake wiped it out. This Kansai of Tanizaki's imagination contradicts the objective reality of Osaka, Kobe and the suburbs between at that time. The region was in fact an entry-point for modern popular culture and imports from the West—cinema, jazz, coffeehouse culture and more. The journalist and cultural critic Ōya Sōichi, for one, marveled at the modernity of Osaka's consumer lifestyle on a return visit to his hometown in 1929, calling it "Japan's America."[2] We do not find that Kansai in Tanizaki's essays.

This imagined Kansai serves as the ground for the remarkable aesthetic statement Tanizaki offers with "In Praise of Shadows." In that essay, he identifies an "Oriental," or Eastern, aesthetics indigenous to Japan and China and sets it against an Occidental, or Western, aesthetics that entered Japan with modernity at the Meiji Restoration. Rooting these opposing aesthetics in purportedly essential qualities of culture, environment and, fundamentally, skin color, Tanizaki argues that Oriental aesthetics values shadow over light, opacity over transparency, duskiness over brilliance, interior over surface. More than simply an aesthetic statement, though, the essay proposes a sort of alternative reality—one in which Japan did not import a modernity made in the West and suited to the West, but rather advanced as a distinct civilization in a different direction, on its own terms. In doing so, Tanizaki makes strange the modernity we thought we knew. The Kansai that Tanizaki imagines in his other essays of the same period is the space of that estrangement. He characterized Kansai as a space outside of time; "In Praise of Shadows" represents a fantastic jump to that imagined reality, the product of an alternate history that de-centers Edo/Tokyo. And by claiming a migrant identity, Tanizaki assumes the role of a traveler to that reality. One scholar has recently suggested that, if "In Praise of Shadows" voices a resistance to modernization, it is to modernization as the erasure of geographical difference and the imposition of supposedly universal rules (on the

East, by the West)—a "modernity-as-spatial-universalism."[3] Tanizaki roots that resistance in Kansai as a stubbornly local place.

Many Western readers have received the aesthetic pronouncements of "In Praise of Shadows" with reverence, but it is worth remembering that an undertone of irony runs through Tanizaki's writings. Should we take at face value his panegyric to the Japanese toilet, for instance, or could he be subtly ridiculing the cultural nationalism that was already ascendent in 1933—and in which his essay participates? His pronouncements depend upon gross cultural and gender-based generalizations. (Reading in the first-floor murk of a century-old Richmond townhouse, I scoffed at the assertion that the roof of a typical Western house—whatever that might be—is "designed to produce as little shade as possible.") That Tanizaki grounds these generalizations in racial essentialism should alert us to read the essay critically rather than reverently. And yet it does reveal, fascinatingly, a certain mindset that modernity produced, and an attempt at "self-ethnography," prompted by dislocation, through which Tanizaki asserts the authority to objectify "the Orient" himself, in the face of objectification by distant, unsympathetic outsiders.

Notes on the translation

In preparing this new translation, I have tried to retain, as much as possible, the rhythm of the original. Tanizaki tended to write long, wandering sentences. And he arranged the sections of the longer essays with very few paragraph breaks. Both previous translations of "In Praise of Shadows" chose to break up the sentences and sections (Starr also gave the sections subtitles), but I have left the sections as Tanizaki wrote them and have done less breaking-up of long sentences.

Tanizaki employs several terms for the metropolitan center of western Japan, around the cities of Kyoto, Osaka and Kobe. "Kansai" (literally, "west of the barrier") contrasts with "Kantō" or "east of the barrier," the broad region around Tokyo. "Kamigata" refers to the traditional culture rooted in the ancient cities of Kyoto and Osaka, in contrast to Edo culture: for example, Kamigata Kabuki as distinct from Edo Kabuki. "Keihan," "Hanshin" and "Keihanshin" are portmanteau terms formed from alternate readings of the first character in "Kyō-to" ("kei"), the second character in "Ō-saka" ("han"), and the first character in "Kō-be" ("shin") and are used rather like the U.S. English term "Bos-Wash corridor" (but more commonly).

All Japanese personal names are given family name first. Titles of Japanese works are given in the original, with English following in parentheses; English titles of book-length works are italicized if a translation of the work is readily available.

M.P.C.

Endnotes

1. These are translated in Thomas Lamarre's edited volume *Shadows on the Screen: Tanizaki Jun'ichirō on Cinema and "Oriental" Aesthetics*, University of Michigan, 2005.
2. Ōya Sōichi, "Ōsaka bunka no Nippon seifuku" (June 1930), in *Ōya Sōichi zenshū,* vol. 2 (Tokyo: Sōyōsha, 1981).
3. Michael Gardiner, "Tanizaki Jun'ichirō's *In Praise of Shadows* and Critical Transparency," *Textual Practice*, 38:7 (2024), 1149.

Hanshin Observations

Hanshin kenbunroku

1925

Osakans are the kind of people who, as a matter of course, allow their children to urinate on the floor while riding a train. Tokyoites will be surprised to hear this, but I assure you I am not exaggerating. I have seen such a spectacle twice. What is more surprising, both incidents occurred not on an inner-city train but on the Hankyu Railway, which is purported to be the line with the most genteel ridership in the Osaka region.

The first time was on a train packed with passengers returning from a performance at Takarazuka of *Dōjōji,* featuring Kikugorō.[1] Hanging from a strap, I heard the sound of someone urinating: *"shaa shaa."* At the same time, I felt some liquid running against my foot. That's strange, I thought to myself, and then, over the heads of several people in the dark and crowded train, I noticed a young mother crouching down and holding a child of three or four. Apart from the unquestionable rudeness of the mother, what surprised me was that neither the train conductor nor the other passengers scolded her or even indicated by their expression any discomfort. Just crouching like that in such a packed car was inconsiderate enough, and everyone in the immediate vicinity must have been splashed by the child, but they all looked completely impassive and unconcerned. One could hardly blame Kikugorō for being disgusted if the audience at Takarazuka consisted of such people. The second experience was again a mother with a young child on a full train car, but this time she was not letting the child urinate but rather defecate. She carefully spread some newspaper on the floor of the train car, had him do his business on it, gathered up the paper, and, carrying it up high over her head past the noses of the other passengers, pushed her way through the crowd and tossed it out the window.

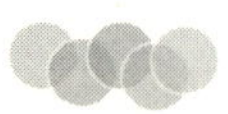

I also recall a young couple in a second-class car of the train from Osaka to Kyoto. They placed their baby, not one year old, on the luggage rack above the seats and, looking up at him, said laughingly, "Now you're riding good and proper!" and so on. Such behavior may be innocent enough, but like the other, more indecent examples, it is a sight one would never see on a tram or train in Tokyo. The mentality of such people is incomprehensible to the common sense of Tokyoites. It feels a bit like observing the customs and practices of a foreign country.

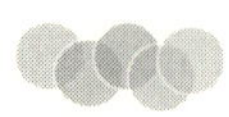

The people of Osaka—even the class of salaried workers, who are supposed to be relatively sophisticated—do not think it at all rude to borrow a newspaper from a complete stranger and start to read it. It is perhaps understandable to do so on a long journey, from the passenger in the next seat, but Osakans' way of borrowing the paper is truly shameless and ill-bred. For instance, when I buy the *Osaka Asahi* and *Osaka Mainichi* evening editions and board the train home, someone immediately sets their eyes on whichever one I'm not reading and comes over to borrow it. Moreover, he comes from a distance, pushing through the crowd, and, as if asking for a light, says "Just borrowing it!" and takes it away with him. Since the car is crowded, I can't see where he's gone, so all I can do is wait, staring into space, until he returns the newspaper. If he doesn't return before we reach my stop, it's possible that I never get it back. It may be just a newspaper, but from my point of view as the lender, it's something I bought and haven't even glanced at yet. I borrow a newspaper only if the other person has finished with it and moved on to the next paper. But no one in Osaka practices such restraint, whether because they are all stupid or because they are shameless.

As for the truly awful sort, I once experienced the following. One evening, I bought the evening editions of the *Osaka Asahi* and *Osaka Mainichi* and boarded a Hanyku train. I'd had a bit to drink and so, as soon as I boarded and got comfortable, I fell asleep. A short while later, someone started shouting in my ear, "Hey! Hey!" I recall that he also gave my shoulder a shake. Just as I opened my eyes, the gentleman stood up, saying "I'll just borrow this newspaper!" "Huh?" said I, rubbing my eyes, still half asleep. But I was wide awake after that, so I thought I might as well read the other newspaper; then I discovered that the gentleman in question had taken both! I was so surprised that I could not recall what the man looked like or recognize him as I looked around the car. The train stopped at Shukugawa, then Ashiyagawa, and finally approached my stop, Okamoto. As I stood up, the man at last returned with my paper. He looked to be a gentleman of about forty, wearing a beard. I'm sure he thought that I would sleep for the whole train ride, and therefore read my papers without concern.

This incident so annoyed me that, from time to time ever since, when I'm feeling cantankerous, I take my revenge. While reading one newspaper, I place the other quite ostentatiously on my lap. Without fail, someone comes over, saying "I'll just borrow this," and I refuse brusquely: "Actually, I'm just about to start reading that one." Then, if they ask for the one in my hands, I say, "I haven't quite finished with it." Once, I intentionally lent my newspaper to someone and then, when I was sure he had read about halfway through the latest installment of a serialized story, I said, "Could I possibly have it back now?" and he reluctantly returned it with a very dour expression on his face. My heart lifted as my everyday resentment dissolved. Nothing else has ever thrilled me as much.

Newsboys come into the train cars at Hankyu Umeda Station to sell the evening edition, so there's ample opportunity to buy a paper. Those who insist upon borrowing someone else's instead of buying their own deserve such severe treatment.

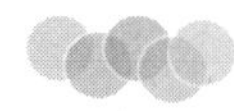

Another thing I've noticed on the train is that, even on a full car with many people standing, those with seats take up more space than necessary. If they would just try to be obliging, one or two others could fit on the bench seat, but no one makes space. If, in frustration, you say, "Can you please move over," everyone gets angry. People with their bag on the seat beside them absolutely refuse to place it on their lap. As the car becomes even more jam-packed, they simply pull the bag a little closer to their side. I think those

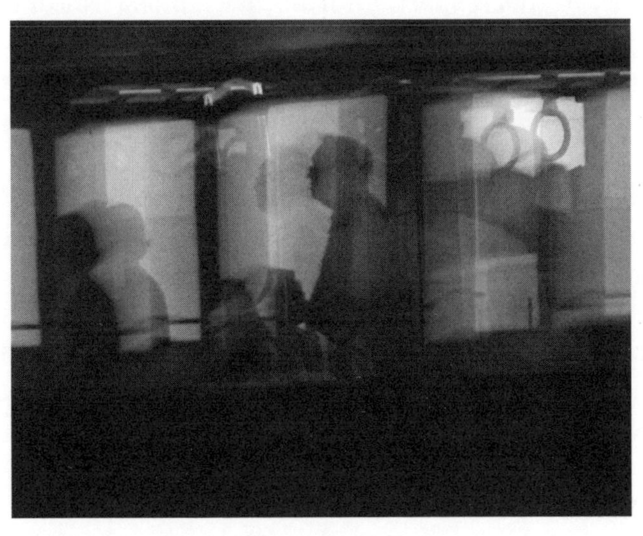

people who silently put up with such behavior are in the wrong. In short, compared with Tokyo, the general populace here is deficient in public spirit.

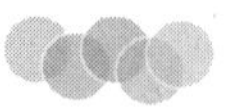

First of all, Tokyoites would never dream of addressing anyone that they do not know at least by sight. It is considered ill-mannered—the sort of behavior expected of a rube. In this respect, Osakans are not as bashful or shy of strangers as Tokyoites are. One could say that they are more candid, and that this is a virtue, but, after all, it strikes Tokyoites as shameless and, even if it's not disagreeable, one still thinks, "How preposterous!"

One morning, I visited the radium hot spring in Kurakuen, at the foot of Mount Rokkō.[2] As I entered the indoor common bath, a young merchant got out of the water and left for the outdoor bath—or so I thought. But then, a young man resembling the first came in, disrobed, and jumped into the bath with me. "Is this the same man as before?" I was wondering, when he grinned and asked, "Hey—aren't you Mr. Tanizaki?" I conceded that I was. "Ha-ha! I knew it! To be honest, I asked at the front desk just now, Is Mr. Tanizaki visiting the hot spring? And they told me, That was Mr. Tanizaki who entered the bath! I wanted to pay my respects, so I came back in."

While that man's behavior may have been lacking in common sense, it was rather charming, too. However, another morning, at the same hot spring, as I was stooping at the edge of the bath and splashing myself, two men sitting in the water stared and talked about me in the rudest manner, right under my nose. "Look! That's Mr. Tanizaki!" one said, and the other replied, "Why, you're right! That *is* Mr. Tanizaki. He's famous, isn't he!" And they gazed at my face in admiration, just as if they were appraising some merchandise. At that point, it would have been better of them to ask, "Aren't you Mr. Tanizaki?" but they absolutely would not address me directly. What a distasteful experience!

Some time ago, I wrote about the cuisine of the Kamigata region, so I thought, this time, I would write about the people. As you see, they are not as superior as the cuisine.

Endnotes

1. Onoe Kikugorō VI (1885–1949) was one of the great actors of the Kabuki stage in the twentieth century. Among his celebrated roles was that of Hanako, the titular maiden of *Kyōganoko Musume Dōjōji* (The maiden at Dōjōji temple, 1753). Takarazuka is a city at one terminal of the Hankyu Railway, developed by the rail company as a resort, with a hot spring and theater.
2. This hot spring closed in 1938, after the Hanshin Flood disrupted the source of radium-infused water.

At Okamoto

Okamoto nite
1929

I fled to Ashiya in September of 1923, after the earthquake. I then moved my household here to Okamoto the following year, on the spur of the moment, and have now been here for six years already. I am honestly surprised at how fast it has passed. I initially had no intention of settling here; I thought Tokyo would probably take at least five years to rebuild, but no more than ten. This would be a place to sojourn until then, I thought. After moving, I traveled back to Tokyo occasionally; but, far from recovering, it grew more and more chaotic, and with the temporary barracks multiplying like wood chips, it seemed unlikely the situation would improve even in twenty years, never mind ten. I lost patience, and so I got comfortable here. I have always enjoyed relocating. I was born in the center of Nihonbashi but moved around repeatedly as soon as I was able to set up a household of my own, starting with Koume in Honjo ward, then Hongō, then Koishikawa, Sōshū-Kugenuma, Odawara and Yokohama, never staying in one place for two full years. But my habitual wandering has finally come to a stop at Okamoto. This is partly due to age, but it is also certainly true that I have grown to like this place. I have built a house facing the western side of the mountain, famous for its grove of flowering plum trees, and I have no desire ever to go home again. My permanent address is still in Kakigarachō, in Nihonbashi, but

I'm thinking to do the paperwork soon to transfer it here to Motoyama. And, since it's a nuisance to travel up to Tokyo for memorial services for my father, I'm even thinking of dividing up his ashes and bringing some to a temple nearby.

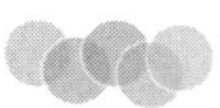

Speaking of temples, I am an adherent of Tendai Buddhism, and my ancestral temple is in Ōjima, in Tokyo, on the banks of the Onagigawa. There's a reference to it in the *michiyuki* scene of the famous Jōruri drama *Akegarasu* (Raven at dawn). In the temple grounds stands the double grave of the lovers Urazato and Tokijirō, from the play. Several years before the quake, the temple relocated to a spot beside the Somei public cemetery and, because of that, it was neither toppled by the earthquake nor burned in the fire that followed. At the same time, it seems that people have mostly stopped visiting the double grave to pray for good luck in love. When I visited the temple this past May to pray for my mother on the twelfth anniversary of her death, the grave was still there, but there were few stupa displayed and very little incense burning. I was overcome with a vague sadness that the traces of the past are gone.

Still, Shiba Kōkan's grave is at this temple, and Akutagawa Ryūnosuke's.[1] In the days of the old shogunate, my grandfather lived in Kamayabori, and the Akutagawa household must have been nearby, in the area of Yokoami, in Honjo.[2] That is why the Akutagawa family gravesite and that of the Tanizaki family stand back-to-back. To be honest, I had not returned to that temple even once since Ryūnosuke's funeral until recently. His monument stands a little apart, in the middle of the Akutagawa plot, and is slightly distinct from an ordinary gravestone. It is a rectangular stone lying horizontally, with a semi-cylindrical top and, on it, carved in heavy bas relief, is "the grave of Akutagawa Ryūnosuke," using his pen name, not his posthumous Buddhist name. Many readers and admirers still visit the grave; in particular, there is one woman who regularly lights incense and leaves flowers—and not only on the monthly anniversary of his death. The priest at the temple said that under no circumstances would he tell me her name.

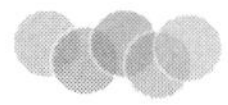

As I think about it now, never in my wildest dreams did I imagine I would come to inhabit this village of Okamoto in Settsu; and when I consider that, but for the earthquake, the chance would never have presented itself, I cannot but marvel at how strange fate is.[3] In my youth I had hoped to live one day in Kyoto, and the first house I rented after the earthquake was in the north of the old capital, near Makino Productions' Tōji-in studios. I lived there with my family for September, October and the first half of November 1923, then moved to a place in the precincts of a temple called Yōbōji, in the Higashiyama neighborhood of Kyoto. It is the head temple of Nichiren Buddhism and appears in the *Karaku meishō zue* (Illustrated famous sights of the capital).[4] In the temple precincts stands one house, built around the remains of an abandoned temple, and I rented the whole thing. A reliquary concealing an icon still stands in the very center of the house, and the footprint of an altar, and so on, so it was a restful place to live, as you might imagine. But, whatever else might be said, the penetrating cold of a Kyoto winter is hard to endure, added to which, the morning sun hits Higashiyama quite late. Even had this not been the case, our daughter, who was of a weak constitution and had become rather high-strung since moving here after the quake, immediately caught influenza. And so, when spring came, we finally pulled up stakes and fled from Kyoto to Kurakuen.[5] We then came to Okamoto at the beginning of April the following year, just as the famous plum blossoms were beginning to fall.

Even now, I am often asked, "Don't you miss Tokyo?" Of course, my family are Edokko, or "children of Edo," on both sides for four or five generations—my father a son of Kanda, my mother a daughter of Fukagawa—and I would love to return if only the old Tokyo were still to be found; but regrettably no trace now remains of that profound "low city" of memory.[6] Perhaps I might still feel some nostalgia if I had been raised in the "high city," since it is little changed even after the earthquake, but Ningyōchō, Kakigarachō, Horiechō and the neighborhood of Suginomori, where my family and our relatives all clustered, burned to the ground, and the city of quasi-barracks that has been built on their ruins shares absolutely nothing with the low city of old— completely alien, even if it resembles it in some ways. If only the street plan remained as it was, but the plot of land in Kayabachō where stood the house I lived in from age seven or eight to fifteen now lies right in the middle of a road that runs to Eitaibashi. Worst of all is the neighborhood near that statue of Fudō in Yagenbori, on the way from Hamachō to Yanokura. The chaos of the street plan there! It is impossibly complicated, with triangular city blocks everywhere. It is difficult for an old Edokko to find his way to Ryōgokubashi without becoming as lost as a child. The more I think about it! My tears fall at the sight, even if I am not Kamo no Chōmei.[7] In the old neighborhoods of Osaka and Kyoto, on the other hand, I still find the Meiji-era architecture, habits and so on that we have already started to forget, and I am reminded of my childhood.

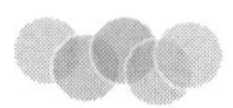

This must be why the families of true Edokko no longer reside in Tokyo's "low city." That reminds me: more and more of the proprietresses of tea houses and houses of assignation now speak the northern dialect. One reason for the decline in the atmosphere of Tokyo after the earthquake is surely the fact that so many people from other regions have moved into the city. The earthquake was a turning point, at which strangers from every quarter invaded the ruins abandoned by locals. And so, culturally, too, today's Tokyo is no longer the same city as before.

The number of locals is also gradually decreasing in Osaka, as residential suburbs are being developed. In that sense, Kyoto is the city that has experienced the least shift in population.

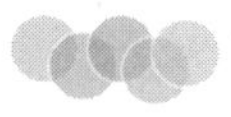

By definition, there are no very old families among the "children of Edo." Most of them came from the provinces of Ōmi, Ise and Mikawa. I do not know if it is recorded in his family record, but Akutagawa's is a historic surname; and if his line descends from the great Akutagawa house of Awa province, then his ancestors were members of the Taira clan. My own surname, Tanizaki, is a very unusual one; there are not many with that name today, nor were there many historically. It cannot, of course, be called a surname of any special pedigree. I only know that my grandfather used to say we had come to Edo from Ōmi five or six generations prior, so probably we descend from Gōshū merchants.[8] When I was young, I used to read the classic war chronicles with great care, to see if the name "Tanizaki" would appear, but I found it only once, in the *Taikōki*, in a passage describing the retinue of Takigawa Kazumasu, where the name "Tanizaki Chūemon" occurs.[9] At any rate, we now know that this Tanizaki became a retainer of the Gamō clan and moved to the village of Hino, in Ōmi. Then, he naturally went with his lord, the daimyo Gamō Ujisato, when he was transferred to Aizu; but some of his family may have remained in Hino.[10] It is impossible to know anything more than this, but Hino is the origin of the Ōmi merchants, and I think the Tanizaki clan had some connection with them. If anyone familiar with the annals of the old families of Gamō county can enlighten me, I would be most grateful.

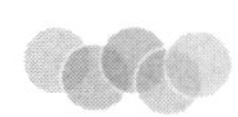

The village of Okamoto is for
easy living; watching the reedy
Ashiya bay, I have woven the year.[11]

Ubara, Sumiyoshi, Ashiya bay
My home looks southward
toward the long view of the ocean.[12]

> When summer comes,
> will my long view of the ocean
> become a bay obscured by leaves?

Lately, I am often asked by individuals to produce some calligraphy. At first, I stubbornly refused, embarrassed at my poor penmanship, but sometimes it becomes difficult to keep saying "No." Nevertheless, when someone thrusts a slip of Chinese paper at me, I simply cannot write anything long, so, in desperation, I determine to sully it with only a short poem. Unfortunately, I never used to write poetry. In fact, I had made a few poor attempts in high school, but had forgotten most of them. I was always copying out the few I did remember, but they were insipid, and so I have begun reluctantly to jot down improvised *tanka*. Printed above are three examples. Regardless of whether they are competent or incompetent, when I am unable to spin an improvised poem, I cheat by writing such prepared things as these, which sing of the place I live now and the life I lead. There is usually some occasion that sparks this sort of pastime, and for me it came one summer, a while ago, when I was selected as a member of the committee to identify "the new top eight sights of Japan" for the *Osaka Mainichi* newspaper and took the ferry from Takamatsu to Tomonoura.[13] I was so moved by the scenery and the delicious food and drink at the lodge there that, when the proprietress produced some slips of paper, I composed poetry for the first time in twenty-odd years:

> Passing a summer night in Tomo,
> on a pillow of waves, will I see
> that person in my dreams this night?

On travels that will not have me pass
a night in Gusu of old,
the lure-fires on the boats at sea.

On a ship circumnavigating Benten's isle,
music and song well up;
dusk at Tomo.

Coming to Abuto peninsula in Bingo of old,
I stand before the Buddha
where no flocking seagulls gather.

Abuto Kannon
who floats on waves,
preserve us in the afterlife!

… and so on; I produced any number of such poorly written verses. And then I temporarily dropped it again until last year, during the rainy season, when I was forced by the rain to linger at the Hototogisu Inn at Saga for two days, where I was handed a small slip of silk and asked, "Please, something as a record of your stay?" I thought and thought as I ground the ink, and wrote the following two poems:

Two nights listening,
not to the cuckoo the inn is named for,
but to the May rain.

At an inn named for the cuckoo,
the water of a mountain stream
near my hangover pillow.

After that, I lost connection with poetry again for over half a year, until this March, when I was asked by the master of the inn where we stayed in Iga Ueno to write something, the night before a visit to the Tsukigase plum grove in Nara.[14] Sitting at the dinner table, I improvised the following:

> Well then, I will lodge here tonight,
> remembering the fragrance of flowers
> I have not yet seen.

It then became a habit, and so the next day, at Tsukigase, I wrote the following poem without being asked:

> Visiting, I neglect
> the plum trees' peak at home:
> the village of Tsukigase.

This is not exactly as I improvised it; I made a few corrections afterward. The original was even clumsier. In any case, I am on board with it now, so, if I have the time, I would like to keep practicing in order to improve.

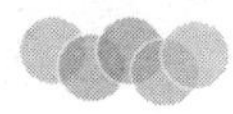

The ancient style of the *Man'yōshū* is currently popular with everyone in the world of poetry, but intentionally mimicking the style of that classic is hard work, I think, though the poems seem simple. Is it not more genuinely naïve to practice at the playful finesse of the *Kokinshū* or the *Shinkokinshū*?[15]

In the first place, in poetry, improvisation and spontaneity are more satisfying than skill, so you should deliver a

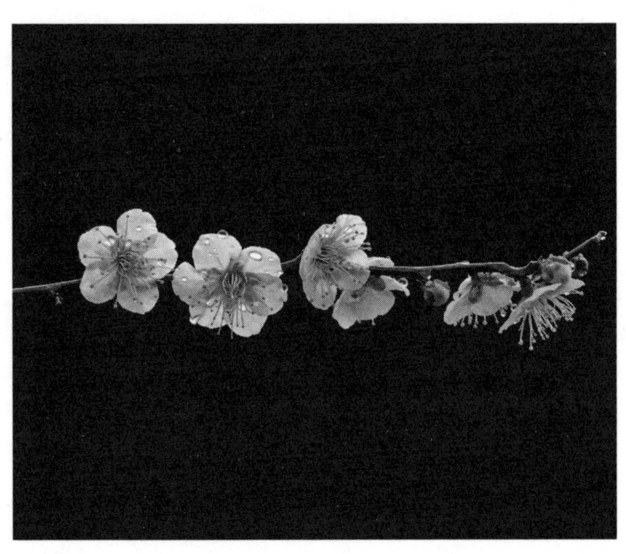

poem as if leaking piss. The poems of Yoshii Isamu (1886–1960) demonstrate what I mean. They rush from one's mouth quite naturally, effortlessly, without the slightest contrivance. There's no hint of artificiality. It comes from the groin, to put it vulgarly. Poetry requires that quality.

Poets of the past—not just those of great talent such as Rai San'yō (1780–1832) and Ryū Rikyō (a.k.a. Yanagisawa Kien, 1703–1758) but perhaps all of them—were so accomplished that impromptu composition was no trouble for them. As for the novelists of that time, however, most were unaccomplished at poetry; they were even more lacking in understanding than the politicians and merchants of the same age. These days, ministers of state and members of the Diet make a nuisance of themselves by brazenly publishing strange Chinese-style poems, but those, like Saitō Ryokuu, who have nothing more to write than "child psychology" are just as much a problem.[16] As far as I have seen, the three Arishima brothers, starting with the eldest and including Mr. Satomi, possess some talent.[17] As for Mr. Mushanokōji, who has recently exhibited some paintings in the Chinese-landscape style, he demonstrates a slightly amateurish charm; for the work of a hobbyist, it is excellent.[18] Young Kitahara Hakushū also draws.[19] Various novelists such as Yoshii, Kubota, Murō and others add poetry to their accomplishments; and whether their calligraphy is skillful or not, they are used to writing on poem slips or colored paper; they link their characters together well, and there is no real possibility of failure.[20] Whereas I am the worst sort of nuisance: someone who, outside of novels, cannot satisfactorily write even a simple letter.

That reminds me of when I was in Shanghai for the first time, more than ten years ago, messing about and staying at the home of an old friend, Tsuchiya Keizō, then the manager of Mitsui Bank's Shanghai branch. He brought out an impressive visitors' book and asked me, please, to write down my impressions or something, as a record of my visit. I declined repeatedly, explaining that I would rather not, since my handwriting is so poor and, in any case, I couldn't think of anything appropriate, but he wouldn't take "No" for an answer. If I didn't mind, he said, I could simply write down the title of one of my novels. There was nothing for it, so, starting with my debut work, I wrote down a catalog of my novels in block letters, but once I had completed it—clumsily, painstakingly—it looked for all the world like a first-grader's handwriting. Sometime after that, Tsuchiya distinguished himself in the Shanghai business world and, as his circle of acquaintances expanded, that visitors' book was graced with the inscriptions of well-known Chinese writers and artists such as Wu Changshuo, Wang Yiting and Qian Shoutie.[21] Thus the disgrace of my poor handwriting was increasingly exposed in China. I do not say this out of false modesty; Wang Yiting apparently said to Tsuchiya, "Why don't you tear out just that page with the ugly inscription?" And still, Tsuchiya brings that visitors' book with him every time he returns to Japan and solicits samples of calligraphy from artists and poets here, so my shame has gradually spread in Japan, as well. Apparently, when Yasuda Yukihiko visited Tsuchiya for the first time and saw my inscription, he said, "I rather respect his nerve."[22] Well, there is really nothing else you could say. When I visited my friend again seven or eight years later, I thought, "The page has probably been torn out by now," but that malicious Tsuchiya was still preserving it, saying, "It's so bad that it makes a good conversation starter!"

Since that is the case, my shame will probably be exposed in Shanghai for the rest of my life.

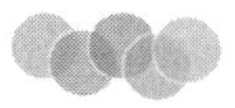

If it comes to that, China is certainly a land of *belles-lettres*. The literary establishment of that country resembles Japan's in the nineteen-teens: suddenly enriched with new novels, dramas and poetry, and the use of punctuation in the Western manner in compositions written in colloquial Chinese. The use of punctuation is even more up to date than in Japan: not only traditional Chinese punctuation marks, but question marks and exclamation points, and even dashes, hyphens, colons and semicolons liberally sprinkled among the kanji. For that matter, even though the literary men among my circle of acquaintances are all quite modern, none would hesitate to write something on a slip of paper or a fan if asked.

On New Year's Eve of 1925, when I was staying at the home of Ouyang Yuqian, Tang Lin, who was then a fresh-faced youth, produced at my request, there and then, the following poem of five characters per line:[23]

> In solitude, the tree in an empty courtyard
> Still flowers as of old.
> One night an east wind rises
> and scatters blossoms in the yellow dust.
> Who would pity the fallen petals?
> Leafy boughs, uneven and untended.
> Alas! If I never see you again in this life,
> Everywhere, the horizon.

That evening, Ouyang also recorded a work he had written earlier:

> Across a bamboo path, empty and cool,
>   shadows travel.
> The fallen petals have turned to dirt, nur-
>   turing the flowers.
> Parrots inadvertently learned the cuckoo's
>   warble.
> Awakened, she adjusts her phoenix hairpin
>   and smooths the hair at her temples.[24]

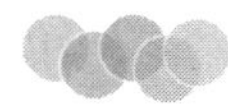

Recently, a certain friend visited and told me that a young woman had asked him to help improve her calligraphy before she married; the writing in the samplers for teaching penmanship in school were too delicate to suit her taste. He thought perhaps to have her practice from Kōetsu's book, but did I have another suggestion? I told him that, unless she possessed an innate aptitude for calligraphy, it would be next to impossible to improve her handwriting using Kōetsu as a model; why not try the work of the Oie style from the Edo period instead? Their early work is excellent, though the brushstrokes grow weak in later generations. Some people joke that it looks like the characters on a paper lantern, and, after all, they are not wrong. But such handwriting is in better taste than the style of the samplers used now at girls' schools. I certainly do not despise that sort of delicate and frivolous calligraphy, but thick, bold, weighty characters can also be charming. And such writing suggests no Chinese affectation at all but overflows with Japanese-style gentility. By practicing from one of the calligraphy samplers of the Tokugawa era, anyone can become reasonably skillful at the paper-lantern-shop style.[25] My friend headed home saying, "The Oie style—that's an idea ..." but I wonder if he went through with it.

Endnotes

1. Shiba Kōkan (1747–1818), painter, printmaker, forger and student of "Dutch studies." Akutagawa Ryūnosuke (1892–1927), influential early-modern author. He and Tanizaki engaged in an important debate, in the pages of literary journals, over plot in the novel.

2. Kamayabori, in Sumida ward, is better known today as Yokojikkengawa.

3. Settsu is the name of the old province within which Okamoto is located. Settsu province occupied parts of what are now Hyōgo and Osaka prefectures.

4. *Karaku meishō zue: Higashiyama no bu* (Illustrated famous sites of the capital: Higashiyama), edited by Akatsuki Kanenari and Kawakita Mahiko, 1859.

5. Kurakuen is an exclusive area of Nishinomiya city in the Hanshin region, between Osaka and Kobe.

6. "Edo" is the former name of Tokyo, before it became the national capital after the Meiji Restoration, in 1868. Edo/Tokyo is conventionally divided into the "high city" (Yamanote) and the "low city" (Shitamachi), roughly according to the areas occupied in the feudal period by daimyo and their retainers, on the one hand, and merchants, on the other.

7. Kamo no Chōmei (1155?–1216), author of *Hōjōki* (*An Account of a Ten-Foot-Square Hut*), which begins with a reflection on the transience of the city.

8. Gōshū was a nickname for Ōmi, itself the name of the old province that occupied current-day Shiga prefecture, east of Kyoto.

9. Oze Hoan's *Taikōki* is a seventeenth-century biography of Toyotomi Hideyoshi (1537–1598).

10. Gamō Ujisato (1556–1595) was an important vassal of Toyotomi Hideyoshi and Oda Nobunaga.

11. The poem puns on the names of two villages near Okamoto: Sumi-yoshi ("easy living") and Ashi-ya ("reeds"). Sumiyoshi was incorporated into Kobe in 1950. Ashiya was incorporated as a city in 1940.

12. This poem again mentions the two villages above and adds an archaic third name, Ubara, a county that was incorporated into Hyōgo prefecture in 1896.

13. Tomonoura is a port in the city of Fukuyama, in Hiroshima prefecture. It is the subject of eight poems in the *Man'yōshū*, the first Japanese collection of poetry.

14. Iga Ueno, in Mie Prefecture, is the site of a famous castle colloquially known as Hakuhōjō, or "White Phoenix Castle."

15. The *Man'yōshū* (completed sometime between 600 and 759), the *Kokin wakashū* (or *Kokinshū*, 905) and the *Shin kokin wakashū* (or *Shin kokinshū*, 1439) are important anthologies of early Japanese poetry.

16. Saitō Ryokuu (1868–1904), author and critic.

17. The brothers are Arishima Takeo (1878–1923), Arishima Ikuma (1882–1974) and Satomi Ton (1888–1983). All three were important figures in the White Birch Society, a literary coterie.

18. Mushanokōji Saneatsu (1885–1976), author and artist, cofounder of a precursor to the White Birch Society.

19. Tanizaki presumably refers to Yoshii Isamu (1886–1960), Kubota Mantarō (1889–1963) and Murō Saisei (1889–1962).

20. Kitahara Hakushū (1885–1942), poet and founding member of the journal *Subaru*.

21. Wu Changshuo (1844–1927), a Chinese calligrapher, painter and carver of seals, known in Japan as Go Shōseki. Wang Yiting

(1867–1938), a.k.a. Wang Zhen, a painter of the Shanghai School, known in Japan as Ō Ittei. Qian Shoutie (1896–1967), a.k.a. Qian Yai, a painter and carver of seals, known in Japan as Sen Sōtetsu.

22. Yasuda Yukihiko (1884–1978) was a progenitor of the *nihonga* style of painting.

23. Ouyang Yuqian (1889–1962), actor, writer and film director, known in Japan as Ōyō Yosen. I have been unable to identify Tang Lin.

24. I am indebted to Xiuyu Li for the translation of these two Chinese poems. Any errors are my own.

25. Specifically, *Onna imagawa* (Precepts for women, 1687) and *Wakan rōeishū* (*Japanese and Chinese Poems to Sing*, c. 1013).

Osaka and Osakans as I See Them

Watakushi no mita Ōsaka oyobi Ōsakajin
1932

Now that Dōtonbori cafes have established their own quarter in Ginza, enticing customers with their Osaka way of doing business, and Tsurugen of Hōzenji Yokochō has opened a branch in a Ginza side alley, the petty resentment that Tokyoites once harbored toward the Kamigata region is fading.[1] But in the last days of the Meiji Era (1868–1912)—that is to say, the days of my youth—there lingered among natives of Tokyo a kind of "Edokko pride," of the sort you find in Rakugo routines about someone sightseeing in the provinces.[2] When the current heads of Shochiku East and West, Messrs. Shirai and Ōtani, bought up stock in the Tokyo Kabuki-za theater and forced out Tamura Nariyoshi, the Eddoko of the fin-de-siecle rose up and protested against Osaka's incursion, with the boys of the fish market taking the lead, hoping to fend off the treacherous scheming of Shochiku.[3] It is still fresh in my memory. Today, there is little such pride to speak of, since Edokko themselves are dying out in Tokyo. However, in a society that tries to preserve some shred of that pride, the genuine Edo traditions have not completely withered. For example, Sadanji and Kikugorō rarely perform on Kansai stages, and when they do, it is at theaters in Kyoto, Takarazuka and Kobe; they almost never visit the small houses around the Dōtonbori.[4] I wonder why. Neither of them is inclined to fussiness, and yet, the tastes and character of

Kabuki actors on the Tokyo stage are extremely typical of the old Edokko type, so the local color and the customs and sentiments of the Kansai region likely offend them. Neither would ever say as much, since their jobs depend on good public relations, but I can more or less imagine how they feel, based on my own experiences.

It seems to have been normal in the Tokugawa era for Kabuki actors to move back and forth between the Kanto and the Kansai stage, but, as for men of letters, I do not know whether there were many—or indeed any—who were born in Edo and moved to Kansai. Hardly any of my close friends have moved here from Tokyo, though many did the opposite. The readiest example is Mr. Shiga, who had a home in Kinugasa, in Kyoto, when he was younger.[5] The year before the Kanto earthquake, he returned to Kyoto and lived in Awataguchi, and now, as everyone knows, he is having a new house built in Nara.[6] As for others, Mr. Kusuyama Masao lived near Nanzenji in Kyoto, and Mr. Osanai Kaoru moved around from Kurakuen, near Mount Rokko, to Tennoji in Osaka, and so on, but neither of them stayed for very long.[7] Just after that earthquake, we witnessed our friends coming to Kyoto, one after another, searching for a safe place to live, but they wanted nothing more than momentary refuge, and before the final aftershocks had subsided in Kanto their numbers were decreasing by one and two until, in no time, all of them had moved back. So it's safe to say that, at present, the only writers from Kanto living here are Mr. Shiga and myself. I recall Shiga once said, "I suppose I will start to miss Tokyo as I grow older"; that makes me feel quite forlorn.

The main reason my acquaintances have abandoned the Kansai region is the difficulty of leading a writer's life outside of Tokyo, so it seems to have nothing to do with the old Edokko antipathy. However, even today it is an undeniable fact that those who were born in Kanto and move here to Kansai must endure the discomfort of feeling like fish out of water—at least for the five or ten years it takes to assimilate to the temperament of people here. Even now I cannot forget how, four or five years ago, I frankly expressed my own antipathy toward the Osaka "type" in an essay titled "Hanshin Observations," published in *Bungei shunjū*, thus incurring the locals' outrage.[8] In my case, however, the local climate and cuisine happily suit my tastes and my constitution better than those of Tokyo. Among my uncles and other relatives are some stubborn Edokko who, when visiting, refuse to eat the white-fish sashimi, barely tolerate the delicately-seasoned simmered dishes, and insist they don't care for the salty local soy sauce, but, as far as my own palate is concerned, I was a Kansai-phile from the start.[9] And by now, far from feeling antipathy toward the so-called *zēroku* disposition, I have developed a sort of affection for it.[10] To be candid, when I moved my family here, we were literally refugees; I intended to sojourn only until Tokyo was rebuilt. What was it, I wonder, that made me put down roots in this soil? I sold my villa at the foot of Mount Rokko last winter and joined the tenant class, but still I have no desire to leave the Kamigata region. Now I am thinking that I will settle here forever, if only it is possible, and will soon bring a portion of my parents' ashes to inter in a nearby temple. I must admit it is a strange fate that a Tokyoite such as myself should form such a bond with this region; at the same time, for better or worse, my affection for the environment and the customs of the Kansai region grows deeper day by day, by a sort of natural logic. And, when it comes to critiquing Kamigata culture based on my observations over the nearly ten years since my arrival in 1923,[11] I insist on doing so not out of the ironical interest I felt when I wrote that earlier essay, but out of affection for the Keihan region, which has now become like a second home. No matter how much time passes, though, I shall never lose the essential temperament of a Tokyoite. Therefore, my observations will, to the end, be made through the eyes of "a migrant from Tokyo." If I occasionally hurl some harsh criticism at the shortcomings of the people of Kyoto and Osaka, it is only out of solicitude for—and as an exhortation to—those upon whose kindness I have trespassed these many years. I beg you, my gentle readers from Kansai especially, to accept it in that spirit.

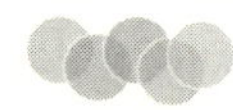

From the beginning, the antipathy that Tokyoites held toward the Kyoto-Osaka region was stronger toward Osaka specifically. Kamigata-haters Sadanji and Kikugorō perform in Kyoto, but they do not lightly come to the center of Osaka. If a Tokyoite who knows nothing about the Keihan region visits here, they might think of living in Kyoto, but they find Osaka truly disgusting. This is to be expected, because no great city except Osaka possesses the might to rival Tokyo (and in this sense people have long subordinated Kyoto; although they say "Kyo and Osaka," there is also an expression, "Kyoto is Osaka's mistress"); Osaka has been viewed as a detested enemy, after all. Because Kyoto is the site of the ancient court and the center of all traditional culture, even the snobbiest Edokko feels some respect and nostalgia for it; moreover, Kyotoites are by nature extremely reserved, so their errors in taste and other faults do not particularly catch the eye of a tourist passing through. Osaka, however, has long been the merchant capital, and because it is in the nature of such people to talk of money before anything else, the temperament of the inhabitants is, on the one hand, dynamic and enterprising, but it is also totally obnoxious, so those defects progressively force themselves upon you. As a result, plainspoken Tokyoites are assaulted, as soon as they disembark at Umeda Station, by a distinct but undefinable *zēroku* odor and are quickly overcome.

It would be pointless to try to explain differences in disposition logically. I believe, however, that the fastest way to understand Osaka-style vulgarity is to look at the stage-names chosen by the actresses in a certain women's theater troupe in Takarazuka.[12] Its stars include Amatsu Otome, Kurenai Chizuru, Kusabue Yoshiko and so on—names that truly reveal the Osaka taste. Here, above all, it seems to a Tokyoite that something is lacking in the Osaka sensibility. At any rate, no Tokyo actress would choose a stage name so shrill, so lacking in refinement—a name like that of a bar hostess, like a brand of cheap and colorful origami paper, like an extravagant pattern on the kimono of the aristocracy, like the previous generation's "new-style" poetry.[13] If even the most celebrated actress in Tokyo were given such a stage name, I can only imagine how her popularity would plummet. When I first moved here, it honestly disturbed me to hear Takarazuka fans—junior high school students and young men—praising such actresses. How dare they brazenly speak names that so set the teeth on edge! What I am writing now is merely a criticism of their stage names, of course. I have not spoken of the various good and bad qualities of the young women who go by these names. It is true that the all-girl revues were once suffused with just the sort of vulgarity suggested by these stage names, but as they have staged "Mon Paris," et cetera, that defect has gradually faded. In fact, as I have gone to see each new program at the revue, I have become a fan. I could wish, though, that they might refine their breathing just a little. As for any advance into the Tokyo market, is it really necessary? I do not know about the Tokyo theaters but, compared with the Shōchiku Musical Opera Company, Takarazuka has more beautiful girls, more perfectly matched, and much more skilled in their artistry; and its costumes, sets and so on are quite expensive-looking and possess an eye-catching brilliance; nevertheless, when it comes to that undefinable *zēroku* odor, Takarazuka is much more pungent. Recently, women here play even male roles, and there is an extreme unnaturalness about it. No matter what they do, it looks like a Kabuki rehearsal, or like the Misaki-za.[14] In addition to that, Kansai ladies have high voices, so when a play has a lot of dialogue, their shrill, piercing tone assaults the ear, making it extremely painful to hear. Even in revues such as "Mon Paris" and "Senorita," when the comic actors perform, the more robust their skills are, the more raucous it gets; what's worse, although those actresses are called "girls," they are in fact women of considerable age, so, with these efforts, they truly seem like the actors of the Misaki-za. Tokyoites watching such a performance may well feel they are going to break out in a cold sweat, but Osakans feel no such embarrassment.

I will not speak flippantly since I have no first-hand knowledge, but it seems to me that a "revue" was originally meant to be a play satirizing the current of the times, so it ought to have a somewhat stinging, spicy flavor. In the Japanese theater's infancy, the operettas staged at the Kannon Theater or the Nippon-kan were extremely coarse, infantile and shabby, but there was something satisfying about them, too, with absolutely no odor of the intelligentsia or the Misaki-za. Since there are Edokko like Mr. Kishida in Takarazuka, such defects are long since recognized, and it is hardly necessary for *me* to point them out.[15] I hear that, starting this spring, numbers with men and women performing together will be added to the program, and, if that is the case, it will cause me gradually to revise my opinion. No matter what, though, I hope that, for the sake of the Takarazuka I love, they at least correct that cloying, overly precious vulgarity.

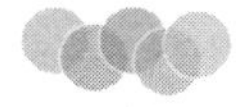

It would be unpardonable of me to keep making an example of Takarazuka, but, while my pen is poised, I will take the liberty of writing a bit more about it. At the Takarazuka Opera Company, they refer to the actresses who appear on that magnificent stage as "students" of the school of musical theater, never as "actresses"; therefore, all of them are treated equally, whether star or extra. One often sees them riding the Hankyu Railway, these unconventional ladies— neither factory workers, nor students, nor girls of good family—wearing Meisen silk kimono over olive hakama,[16] the hem 8 or 9 centimeters too short, revealing white *tabi* socks and, usually, *geta* (sometimes *zōri*, but, in that case, certainly without *tabi*),[17] hair done up in pigtails or perhaps a chignon. The youngest are 16 or 17 years old, the oldest close to 30, traveling together in twos or threes, or sometimes groups of four or five. This is the uniform the students of the musical-theater school wear when going out, as everyone living in the neighborhoods along that line knows, and it has become part of the scenery of the Hankyu Railway. Seeing these girls dressed so dowdily, it is hard to imagine the beautifully proportioned limbs and torsos beneath those clothes, and the loveliness of those magnificent, slim legs. At any rate, nothing else more richly reveals the local color of Osaka. Presumably, the Takara-zuka purposely makes these girls present themselves in this unfashionable manner to train them as proper students of the opera company: sweet, refined and as pure as possible. In those modest uniforms, they feel no need to compete with one another over the extent of their wardrobe; moreover, they are treated relatively well, and so their conduct is certainly irreproachable, especially compared to the "actresses" of other theater troupes. And yet … in Tokyo, if you made a girl wear such oafish clothes, it would probably hurt her popularity; and a slightly impertinent star would absolutely never stand for it. It may be that, in such circumstances, the unaffected, mild, gentle nature of the Kamigata woman clearly manifests itself. A dancer or singer in a revue ought to be quite smart and chic, but that extends only to her presentation and posture on stage; off it, this austere uniform utterly lacking in any modern taste may, on the contrary, be considered somehow decent.

As I write this, it suddenly occurs to me: those girls in the olive hakama look just like *hina* dolls of court ladies![18] There are a great number of these students, so there are some of the Clara Bow type, with a round, animated face, but, if I had to say which, there are more faces of the

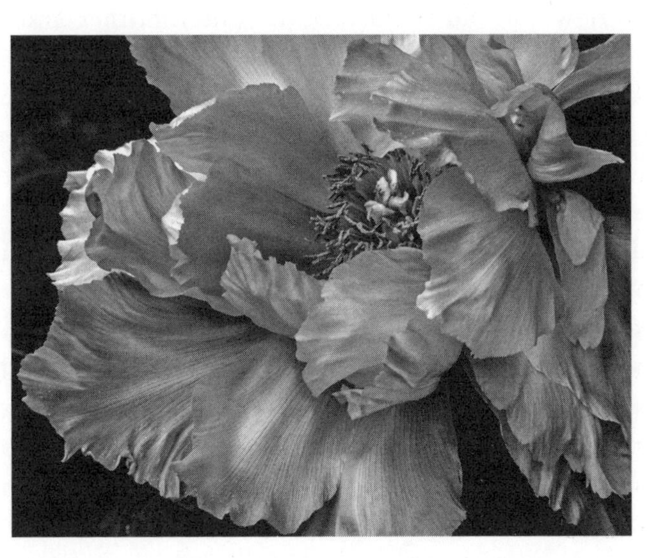

princess type: long with prominent features, as Kunisada[19] drew faces. This is evidence that, in the Kamigata region, people still esteem traditional beauties like those depicted in art; you understand this clearly if you look at the face of, for example, the tennis player Miss A, who is rated the leading beauty of the Kansai women's sports world.

I am somewhat acquainted with Miss A and would not dispute that she is a beauty; and then, her princess-like quality rather suits her situation in life. But she combines both new and old society, both contemporary and traditional style, and, in general, there are many with her sort of beauty, and even those without that sort of face make themselves up to look that way. For this reason, the students at the Takarazuka theater school, when they are appearing on stage, paint the bridge of their nose especially white and take effort to make their features look slightly too prominent. That would be unobjectionable in a Japanese drama, but it is, of course, inappropriate to a Western-style revue. It looks as though the head of a court lady has been affixed to the torso of a French doll. The reason I am partial to Sumino Saeko is that, in addition to the beauty of her arms and legs, I have noticed a unique quality in the contours of her face; but even Saeko has the habit of heavily painting her nose, and of this I strongly disapprove. After all, there are round-faced beauties in the Kamigata region, too, and I would have women with that sort of face make the most of their idiosyncratic looks.

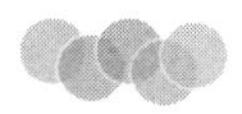

My friend Nagano Sōfū has a theory that, if you walk around the town of Kyoto, you will repeatedly catch sight of faces exactly like those of the common people depicted in ancient scroll paintings, and he says that this demonstrates how accurately the images in those scrolls were drawn from nature.[20] Anyone may notice this, though they are not an artist like Sōfū, if they just take a little care to observe. Comparing Tokyoites and Kyotoites one by one, there is no special difference between the people of the two cities, but if one comes to the Kansai region and looks at the appearance of citizens walking along the streets, one is indeed struck by the sorts of faces that one never sees in Tokyo. Those faces carry a trace of centuries past—so much so that, were you to strip those people of their *haori* jackets, their Inverness coats, their business suits and so on, and dress them instead in the costumes of Heian aristocrats or ancient court robes, place straw hats on the women or arrange their hair in the style of the Edo period, a street scene from an ancient illustrated scroll would emerge.[21] This is more the case in Kyoto than in Osaka. If the former is home to faces like Noh masks, however, those of the latter suggest the venerable age of Rakugo puppets. In the faces of Kyoto still linger the ancient traces of the Nara, Heian and Kamakura periods. That is not to say that one cannot sense a certain premodern flavor—at least of the Keichō, Genna, or Genroku periods—in the faces of Osaka, too.[22]

Perhaps that is why Osaka ladies never quite look smart in Western-style outfits. Walking recently in the neighborhoods of Shinsaibashi and Umeda, in Osaka, I occasionally saw a splendid "modern girl" with not a single deficiency in her clothing or accoutrements, but most of these were Tokyo women visiting the city.[23] As to the most fashionable district in Kansai, that is the area along the Hankyu Railway between Shukugawa and Mikage. The young wives and daughters living there have a good eye for Western clothes and a growing taste for them, and since money is no object, their choice of furs, gloves, handbags and so on is faultless. And yet, they somehow lack chic. To be clear, they certainly do not look provincial or shoddy. As for elegance, they are unfailingly elegant. But try as they may, just like the Takarazuka girls I mentioned, they cannot avoid a precious quality—the look of a Japanese princess donning Western clothes. Indeed, even when wearing kimono, the women of Kansai coordinate colors in a much gaudier way than do the women of Kanto. Those loud colors certainly harmonize wonderfully with the scenery along the streets of the Hanshinkan, so typical of warm climes: the deep blue sky, the verdure of the pine groves, the dazzling white sand. That taste for the gaudy becomes a bit problematic, though, when transferred from a kimono to a crepe-de-chine dress.[24] It may not be the women's intention; perhaps even now they dress this way unconscious of the influence of climate and landscape. At any rate, to my eyes, the sense of an elaborately patterned kimono clings to these Kansai ladies' Western-style clothes. The colors are incomparably pretty and gay, but the clothes are too delicate, too dainty; they might as well be wearing a silk crepe under-kimono, because they are missing the most essential quality—what we might call the "esprit" of Western fashion. It is rather the mixed-race office girls around Kobe who sport the true Western fashion, even in a simple blue serge.

It is not only their way of coordinating colors; it most certainly has a lot to do with their build and movement. The *genius loci* of Kanto has always been uncivilized, and even the women there delight in everything vigorous. This conforms readily to the current flapper mentality, and there is a danger of assimilating the American manner in matters of comportment and expression. On the other hand, though the people of Kansai were to adopt Western clothes, would we not know them by their deportment, saturated as it is in centuries of refined habit? During my childhood in Tokyo's "low city," when one never saw a woman in anything like Western dress, it was common for young women to roll up their sleeves. My mother would roll the sleeves of her summer kimono up to her shoulders and cool herself with a round fan. It was the sort of thing a mature woman in her twenties or thirties might do, flaunting the pale skin of the fleshy upper arms as in a woodblock print by Yoshitoshi. In that way, it was no different from today's women wearing a summer dress to show off the muscular beauty of their well-developed limbs.[25] This dashing style no doubt originated with the geisha in the Tatsumi quarter in Tokyo before it came to be imitated, little by little, by the wives and daughters of respectable merchants. I doubt that anyone in the Kyoto-Osaka region ever adopted such an unladylike fashion—certainly not "Madam" and "the young Miss," and perhaps not even geisha there. As a result, even the young women of today's Osaka, who are raised to wear Western clothes from the time they enter school, are unwittingly influenced by their mothers and older sisters at home, and naturally those habits are evident even when they dress in Western styles. Honestly, young women in Western clothing should give the sensation of a voluptuous body packed into their clothes—of clothes billowing over with stuffing. This is precisely the quality to which applies the word "it," so in vogue right now, but there is not the least such quality in the ladies of Kansai society. Their legs and ankles are shapely, of course; they generally do not look like daikon radishes. On the other hand, the line from the lower back to the buttocks is overly delicate and forlorn; moreover, each time they walk, their hips sway and their upper body beats in pliant waves as their bust makes its way before them. When you watch a Western woman from behind as she walks, you clearly see the flexing and relaxing flesh of the buttocks, left and right, and the trunk rides firmly on the big pelvic bones; but there is little feeling of fleshiness in Kansai women; their skirts flutter loosely around the buttocks. This may also be due to their delicate physique and mincing gait. And yet Kansai women change their get-up almost every day: yesterday, felt sandals with a silk brocade formal kimono; today, high-heeled dancing shoes with a French silk evening gown. They take pains to differentiate even their way of walking depending on whether they are wearing Japanese or Western clothes. And yet, the flirtatious and strangely pliant manner of, for example, the movement of their heels and their duck-toed walk is somehow leisurely and redolent of Japan. In short, their figure in Western clothes is never less than elegant, but the clothes are gaudy and flimsy, and the women make a weak impression, as though they might fall over if you suddenly gave them a shove.

On the other hand, schoolgirls in Western clothes are shockingly rude and filthy. I am not well-informed about the behavior of Tokyo schoolgirls in recent years, but even dressed in their all-navy uniforms they seem to be lacking something. As for Osaka schoolgirls, except for those of a few special schools they differ little from schoolgirls in the provinces. Dressed in Western clothes, they look no different from tenement housewives or kitchen maids. They seem already to be insisting on convenience and practicality, completely disregarding anything like feminine attention to appearance. Of course, it does not do for a girl still of school age to be too concerned with fashion, but can she not take a little care to maintain herself and dress smartly? Can she not avoid becoming unkempt, and notice when her socks are wrinkled and smooth them out? I think it might be necessary for the appropriate person at school to at least teach them how to brush and iron their clothes, for the sake of modern womanhood. If they are like this in their school years, surely it will be impossible for them, upon graduating, to suddenly begin wearing Western clothes with any chic.

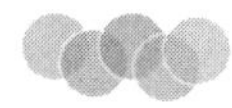

Nothing so strongly impresses upon me the difference in the temperaments of Osakans and Tokyoites as the way they use their voice. It is in the voice, more than the words, that the distinction between east and west emerges most clearly. The gap between the Kamigata dialect and the Tokyo dialect will likely disappear as intercourse between the two regions steadily increases, but I think it will be difficult to eliminate the differences in the tone of voice produced from the throat—probably because it has to do with the air, geography and climate of each region. When, on occasion, I visit Tokyo now, having lived so long in Kansai, what immediately makes me feel, "Now, *that's* Tokyo!" is the desiccated voice in which locals speak. I say this although I probably speak in the same way myself; but to ears grown accustomed, from constant exposure, to the voice in which Osakans speak, Tokyoites' pronunciation sounds to me harsh, lusterless and exceedingly bleak—just like Tokyo's infamous cold, dry wind. With men, that also means that they enunciate clearly, in a positive sense. But when a woman produces that voice, it gives an extremely hardened effect, and I come to think of its possessor, herself, as a coarse, thick-skinned sort of person.

Among Tokyo Kabuki actors, it is Kikugorō whose technique the people of Keihan find most difficult to warm to (apart from his *Buyō* dancing); perhaps they are most put off by the pure Edo style of his vocalization. Whereas Sōjūrō, who is rather unpopular in Tokyo, does not have the same problem in Kamigata, and I am sure it is because of his voice.[26] That cloying, lazy drawl is detested by Tokyoites, but the people of Kamigata cannot understand what makes it so objectionable. Though Kōshirō, Kichiemon and Ennosuke are also Tokyoites,[27] they each have their own exaggerated way of producing their voice, and Sadanji has a characteristically harsh and decisive quality.[28] But the voice Kikugorō employs for dialogue in the plays about townspeople reproduces exactly the voice that Edokko in the streets used in their everyday lives; having heard it a little, I find it quite brusque and hard to grasp. Uzaemon can be rather blunt too, but not like Kikugorō.[29] *His* voice sounds effortless but is really a product of the kind of technique that only Kikugorō possesses. Still, Osakans do not readily appreciate its charm. If that voice is extremely frank and curt, the Osaka voice is sometimes overly guttural, and Tokyoites are revolted when they hear it, feeling an unbearable discomfort well up within them. The other day, I read, in some magazine or other, an article in which Tsubouchi-sensei criticized the performance style of Soganoya Gorō, and while I could not help but agree with the drift of his argument, I think the main reason Tokyoites find Gorō too vulgar is his over-expressive voice—like that of a cinema *benshi* or *naniwabushi* singer—by turns husky, hoarse, sonorous, sticky and syrupy.[30] As an experiment, I think it would be useful to compare his voice to that of a modern *shinpa* actor such as Kitamura.[31] While the latter speaks clearly, in crisp, brisk, ringing tones, the former makes vulgar noises like vomiting; when I try listening to him, his vocal fry reverberates in my inner ear like a constant rumble. Gorō's vulgarity stood out even more when he was appearing for a while with the late Jūrō, because Jūrō had a light voice and a clever, witty turn of phrase. In truth, Gorō seemed to be an unpleasant actor. The Rakugo raconteur Harudanji likewise produces that gravelly voice.[32] Bunraku narrators, not surprisingly, have mastered the art of prettifying that voice, rendering it not unpleasant to the ear. In truth, just about everyone in Osaka can do that voice; each has their own manner of speaking in ordinary conversation but in an argument or quarrel, when they put energy behind their words, their voice inexplicably changes. I have felt the shocking incongruity of hearing a pale young milquetoast, who ordinarily speaks in a girlish whisper, produce that voice on some impulse. Indeed, it is not only men; to my surprise, even women speak that way. More than once, I have been shocked to hear that low, gloomy voice emerge from the seductive throat of a young lady in the bloom of youth.

Come to think of it, in Osaka, it is not unusual to find a women with a deep natural voice, like a wide-neck shamisen played by a geisha.[33] To look at such a woman, you would expect her to possess a jewel-like high, clear voice, but engage her in conversation and out comes a sound like a goose. I cannot help feeling sorry for them. In fact, I know two or three such ladies. I suppose you might find them in Tokyo, too, if you searched, but none comes to mind, so they must be extremely rare.

Another thing: rolling one's "r"s is thought to be a particular characteristic of the Edo dialect, but that is not the case. I have never heard people from Kyoto do it, but when Osakans use the rolled "r" to say, for instance, "I oughta r-r-r-rap you one!" their voice weirdly slithers up and coils around you like a snake. To me, the Osaka rolled "r" sounds far more terrifying than that of Edo.

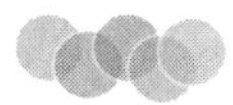

I brought up only the disadvantages of the Osaka voice in the preceding paragraph, but of course it has many advantages, as well. And, as for myself, I find the Osaka voice more beautiful, overall, than the Tokyo voice. Considering the issue impartially, though it may be fifty-fifty with the men, when it comes to the women, I must award victory to Osaka.

Even with the women, the goose-like, deep voice and the thick, *naniwabushi*-style voice are problems, but not all of them sound like that. It is safe to say that seven out of ten Osaka women possess lovely voices. I never used to pay special attention to the pronunciation of Japanese, except when listening to actors speak their lines, but I have really noticed it since coming to Osaka and hearing the everyday speaking voice of ladies here. The language used by the women of Kyoto has long been renowned for its gentleness, but Osaka is even gentler in this regard than Kyoto. Kyotoites' pronunciation has a certain mellowness, compared to that of Tokyoites, but it is still not as sweet as Osakans'. So, while Kyotoites avoid the unpleasantness of the guttural voice I mentioned before, they also lack charm. If I am forced to decide, I think the most beautiful women's voices are those in the area from Osaka to around Banshū.[34] If you continue west or south from there, strange accents and sing-song intonations enter the local speech and pollute it. I have come to believe this after having an opportunity to hear the voices of I know not how many young women from the domains between Osaka and Kyushu who have come to my house to work as live-in maids over the past decade. I recall two girls that worked at our Okamoto house, one from Imazu, in nearby Settsu, and the other from a prefecture next to Tokyo.[35] When they started working together, the sharp, cold tone of the Kanto girl's voice struck my ear in such a strange way that I not only found it difficult to listen to her but, in the end, through no fault of her own, I ended up hating her.

The shamisen offers the best analogy for understanding the difference in voice between eastern and western Japan.[36] Indeed, it is no coincidence that shamisen with a bright tone—of the sort used to play *nagauta*—were developed in Tokyo. The voice of Tokyo ladies has the same timbre as that *nagauta* shamisen, for better or worse, and truly complements it. If you want to call it pretty, yes, it is pretty; but it has no range, no depth, no warmth and, above all, no stickiness. Their conversation, likewise, is precise, articulate and grammatically correct, but lacks any lingering charm, any suggestiveness. The Osaka voice, on the other hand, is like the sort of shamisen developed there for the Bunraku and Kamigata folk songs: no matter how high the pitch goes, that voice retains its wetness, luster and warmth. If we compare them to Western instruments, the Tokyo voice is like a mandolin—or, in the worst cases, like

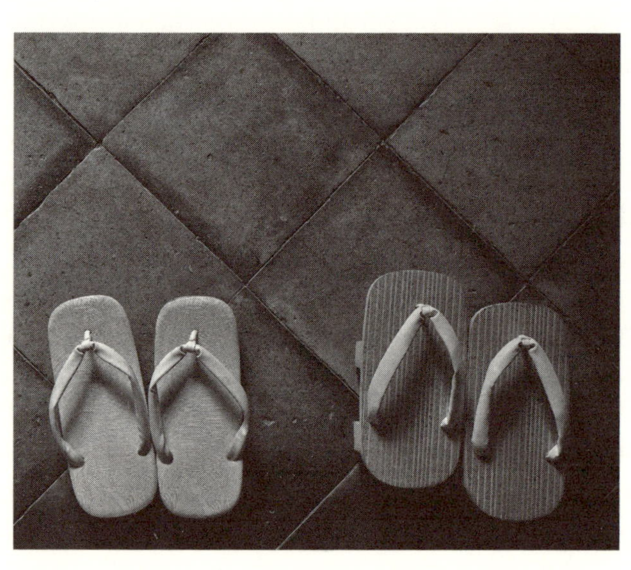

a Nagoya harp—while the Osaka voice is a guitar. It is my pet theory that a Tokyo woman is interesting for everyday conversation, while an Osaka woman has the right disposition for pillow talk. In any case, apart from any sexual interest, when a Tokyo lady engages in a war of words, with the sort of attitude she might take against a man, she will be bold and crude, presumptuously sarcastic and captious, so she is a worthy opponent. However, the Osaka lady possesses feminine charm and allure. In short, to me, the Tokyo woman does not give a womanly impression.

I do not mean to suggest that Osaka women are lewd or vulgar. It is rather Tokyo women who are crude, given that they are outspoken, impudent and wanton, somehow giving the impression of brazen hussies. Although the practice is unknown among the nobility and peerage living in Tokyo's Yamanote area, who still speak the Kyoto dialect, the so-called upper classes in Tokyo now intentionally mimic the style of the lower classes, so that elegance and refinement are disappearing, little by little. Our discussion is shifting from "voice" to "language," but I especially hate the Tokyo *asobase* idiom.[37] It is fine if used in moderation, but when it reaches the point of affixing "*asobase*" to every word, one after the other, spoken in an impatient rush without pausing for breath, such a roundabout locution is preposterous! Nothing is less elegant than straining for elegance in this pretentious and affected manner. Compared to that, the patois of the Osaka docks or Kyoto's Gion entertainment district sounds more graceful and refined. Long ago, the *asobase* idiom probably did not sound so unpleasant and insincere; I suppose it is the fault of lady educators that the idiom has become so degraded. One nice thing about Osaka is that you hardly ever hear it here, even in the highest circles of society. If, on occasion, some-one uses it, that person is either an immigrant from Tokyo or a schoolteacher who is crazy for Tokyo.

One can appreciate the quality of a Kamigata lady's voice by asking her to sing something to *koto* accompaniment. While I lived in Tokyo, I thought there was nothing so dull and monotonous as the sound of the *koto*, but that was the fault of the ladies of Tokyo. It goes without say-ing that the sort of voice appropriate to *dodoitsu* or *hauta* comes off poorly when forced to adjust to the timbre of classical instruments.[38] When an Osaka woman sings to *koto* accompaniment, the timbre of the strings and the natural voice sustain a subtle harmony, even amid the mo-notony, and a mood wells up, faint yet warming. When listening to someone with an exceptionally beautiful voice, one thinks: "This must be the sort of voice in which a young lady of rank recited poems in days of old, secluded behind the waterfall at Tamadare," and it calls up dim vi-sions of a dignified court lady in an under-kimono. Judg-ing by their voices, the blood of tradition flows thick in the veins of Osaka ladies.

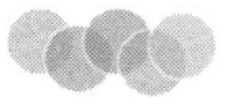

Self praise is no praise, but to be honest, I have taken pride in my voice ever since I was young. In the teahouses, peo-ple used to encourage me to chant short ballads or long ep-ics that I had learned by heart; but these days, when I try to learn a folk song, somehow my voice does not come out as I expect it to. It sounds husky on the high notes and oddly strained on the low notes. I thought it must be largely the effect of age, but even now I can sing as freely as I used to if it is an Edo song. That really brought home to me the fact that the source of the voice is different for Edo songs and Kamigata songs. When a Tokyoite, whoever it is, sings a song from the west—even such minor folk songs as *yasugi bushi* or *kushimoto bushi*—they perform the melody like someone slurping down tea-and-rice, and it lacks charm.[39] That sort of song simply does not work without the sticky Kamigata-style voice, all tangled up with the tongue. The same can be said about Osaka geisha performing Edo-style Jōruri or ballads. Nothing about the melody is incorrect, so it is impossible to point out what exactly is wrong, but the enunciation is slurred and the vocal "digging" insufficient, so that, somehow, it lacks that "Edo" feeling. The single exception is Koutsubodayū,[40] who, though a Tokyoite, tried to build upon the legacy of Tsudayū, but even in his case there may be something missing for listeners with the ears to hear it.[41] I suppose that, even if he has acceded to the same crest, it is difficult to attain the level of such masters as Settsu and Koshiji.[42]

I mean to say, why is Edo-style shamisen music currently conquering Kansai, while few people there try to learn the arts of their own region, such as the *koto* music of the Ikuta school, or local folk songs? Even in my own neighborhood, here and there I can catch the sound of a shamisen playing *nagauta* or *kiyomoto*, but I hardly ever hear the *koto* or the thick-necked shamisen. Granted, *nagauta* is fine, since the singer produces the voice in an unaffected way; but recently *kouta* is enjoying another boom. Even among Edo-style songs, *kouta* has an especially deep Edo quality, and an extremely frivolous, decadent air. Of course, that sort of thing does not appeal to most people, even many Tokyoites; if we compare *nagauta* to waka, then *kouta* is like haiku. It is hardly likely that Osakans could master that style of singing or fully appreciate its mood. And regarding classical dance, too, it is terribly sad to see the Yamamura and Inoue schools, of Osaka and Kyoto, becoming obsolete, overtaken by the Fujima and Hanayagi schools of Tokyo. While there is no reason needlessly to raise the complicated issue of local art forms, when I consider the instinctive, innate and unbreachable difference between the peoples of Kansai and Kanto, I have good reason to want to unsettle Osakans on this point.

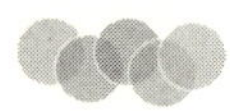

Takebayashi Musōan once said, upon returning to Japan after a long stay in France, "For Parisians, there is a single prescribed formula to everyday life, but there is no such thing for Tokyoites; truly, it is chaos."[43] Although such a formula was present there in my childhood, sure enough, it has now largely disappeared.

What is meant by "a formula for everyday life"? It is a standard set of conventions that arises naturally over time in one family or society: an annual cycle of events. Decorating with pine branches at the New Year, celebrating the Doll Festival in March, raising the *koi-nobori* banner for Boy's Day in May, exchanging red beans and rice with relatives at the Spring and Autumn equinoxes, and so on. And in families, too, certain acts are performed over and over again, starting with the time everyone rises in the morning and goes to sleep at night, the time they pray before the ancestral tablet each morning and evening, the times of their three meals, and the place of each family member at the table; and then, as the seasons turn, certain fish and vegetables appear on the table at the same time each year.

In addition, I need hardly mention the clothes and the phrases proper to happy and sad occasions; the household decorations for festivals; the folding screens, carpets and curtains. In Tokyo, each family once had certain places they visited regularly every year on excursions to see the cherry blossoms, or the chrysanthemum displays, or the autumn leaves: Mukōjima or Asukayama in spring, Dangozaka or Takinogawa in fall; and, returning from Dangozaka, they would stop at the Matsugen restaurant in Ueno, or, returning from Mukōjima, at Manbai in Asakusa. On such occasions, our father and mother would dress every year in the same outfits—their best—so that the mere sight of those clothes and their scent vividly called forth fond memories of past excursions. I suppose that the citizens of Paris, too—not visitors but those who have lived there for some decades—are probably thrifty, hard-working and reserved, seldom ordering new clothes or the like, their lives similarly fixed, rotating their wardrobe with the seasons, bringing out the same clothes year after year, down to the hats, cloaks and gloves, and taking the same route to work or for a stroll day after day, dropping in at the same café or restaurant.

I am not suggesting that this sort of prescribed everyday life is good or bad. Today's younger generation must disdain such practices as bourgeois pastimes of the Meiji era. In any case, all of that is dying out in contemporary Tokyo. Only a few customs remain, such as pine decorations at New Years. Even when it comes to the Doll Festival, households that don't celebrate it certainly outnumber those that do. This is because, first of all, Kanto's culture is still young compared to Kansai's. And then, Kanto's geology is such that it is frequently visited by destructive earthquakes, so there is no time for certain customs to take root properly. Nevertheless, prescribed forms of everyday life are by no means limited to those of the Meiji-era bourgeoisie. If the mores of the past are disagreeable, new ones can be made.[44] Originally, Tokyoites were more alert than Osakans to trends of thought and fashions from abroad, but now each household goes in its own direction—some adopting the French manner, others the American, and, since it is often no more than a brief infatuation rather than a lasting influence, they change continually, so that no mutual standard is established in society at large. On the contrary, society becomes more and more disordered, and everyone behaves just as they wish. Consider the celebration of Christmas, for instance; setting aside the argument that it is absurd for a non-Christian people to observe the holiday, if that becomes a widespread custom in Japan, then I think it might reflect a deeper sentiment. Still, I cannot help wondering how much longer it will continue and how much more widely it will spread. Tokyoites are likewise quite chaotic in their dress. The Russian *rubashka* blouse was once fashionable among literary youths and actors; after that, many walked around in Chinese-style outfits; and now both those styles have fallen into obscurity.

Meanwhile, in Kansai, the prescribed forms of everyday life of which I speak are being completely preserved—by the inhabitants of the old neighborhoods of Kyoto and Osaka, of course, but also in the new commuter suburbs of the Hanshinkan. Though it is crowded with modern, red-roofed houses, the lives of the inhabitants are by no means as Westernized as the architecture would suggest. This is because many of them moved there from the finest neighborhoods in Osaka—Senba, Nakanoshima and the like—or

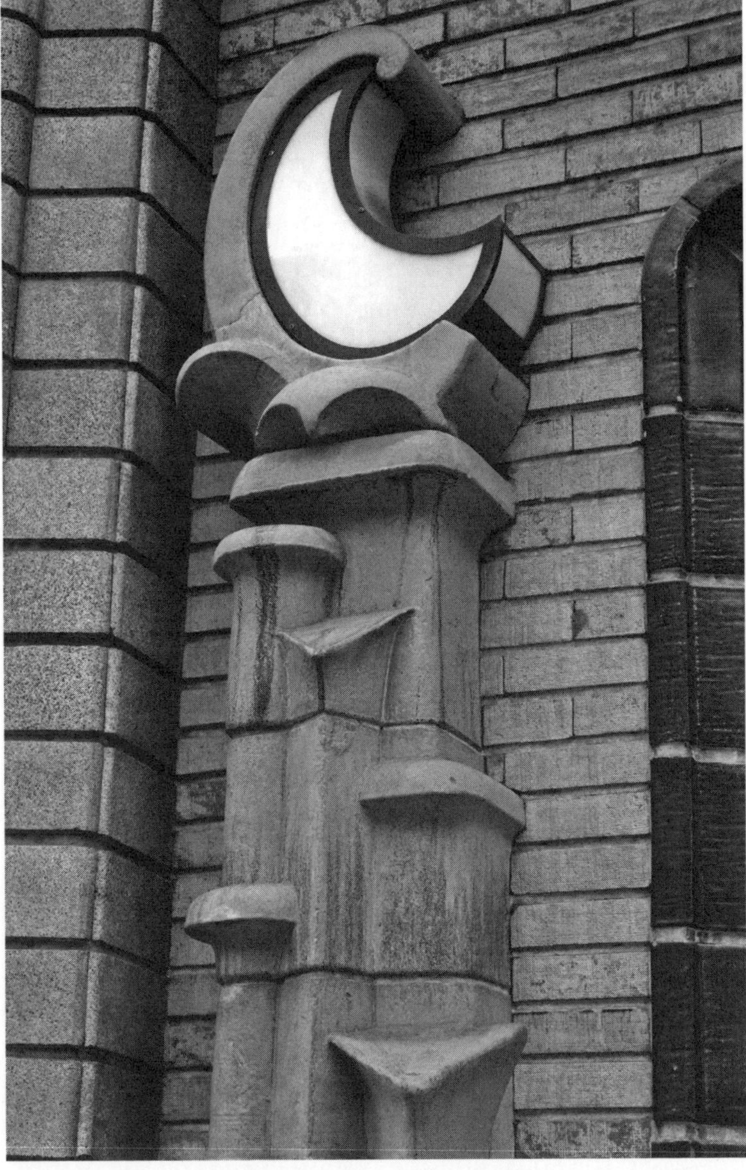

else they are wealthy farmers or landowners, most of them. And so, on the one hand, they occupy a modern-style mansion and live there in a comfortable manner while, on the other hand, they hold fast to the mores of their old, established families. I will offer just a small example: when exchanging letters, the families living along the Hankyu line still ordinarily put their correspondence in a box decorated with the family crest and give it to their maid to deliver by hand. It is not only the elderly and old-fashioned who do so; even young wives and daughters of good family—the sort who attend balls—will secure their letter in a lacquer box decorated in gold and have it hand delivered, though it be the sort of private note delicately inscribed with a fountain pen and tucked into a perfumed envelope. I, too, often receive this sort of letter. Apart from these, seasonal greetings at the Bon festival and New Year's, gifts to the servants and so on are all handled very properly. Once, when my daughter brought a gift to her elementary-school teacher's home, that teacher gave my daughter 30 *sen*. It would seem almost insulting in Tokyo, but it is apparently established custom in Kansai to give a "tip," however trifling, to any go-between. Moreover, one never hands such a tip, whether small or large, to the recipient directly; rather, one inserts it in a special envelope for cash, then either wraps it in a letter of reply or places it in a correspondence box and brings it to the head of the household, who then hands it to a servant. Considerable care goes into such proceedings.

It is not in fact the case that, just because Osaka is thoroughly a merchant capital, it developed no complicated system of etiquette such as existed among the samurai class. Those wealthy merchants who, though commoners, possessed the spirit and the resources to rival the daimyo insisted upon their own dignity and observed the distinction between master and servant as carefully as daimyo did, as one might expect, and were extremely fussy about, for example, the relations between the main house and a cadet house in a clan. So even now custom dictates how to respect a house's social standing, and custom haunts important ceremonial occasions, one after the other. In Osaka firms of long standing, a head clerk, after working for a certain number of years, will be granted a "division of the shop curtain" (*noren-wake*) and permitted to open a branch shop. That shop will then occupy a position vis-à-vis the main shop similar to that of cadet branch of an aristocratic clan, and the main shop will look after the branch shop for generations, assuming responsibility even for the wedding expenses of the clerk's daughters. This sort of custom will certainly die out as modern forms of business organization spread. Nevertheless, present-day Osaka boasts more well-established independently owned firms than Tokyo, and so, correspondingly, such conventions still obtain. In one old family I know, there are as many as twenty branch houses that depend upon the main house. On New Year's Day, all twenty branch houses assemble and line up in the great hall of the main house. The master of the main house then offers his best wishes for the new year to each of them according to seniority and passes each of them a celebratory cup of sake in turn. On the fifteenth day of the new year, a similar ceremony is held between the mistress of the main house and those of the branch houses. On that occasion, the mistresses of the branch houses wear outfits they have received from the mistress of the main house: black twill kimono decorated with the house crest and tied with a black satin sash. Although many of those main

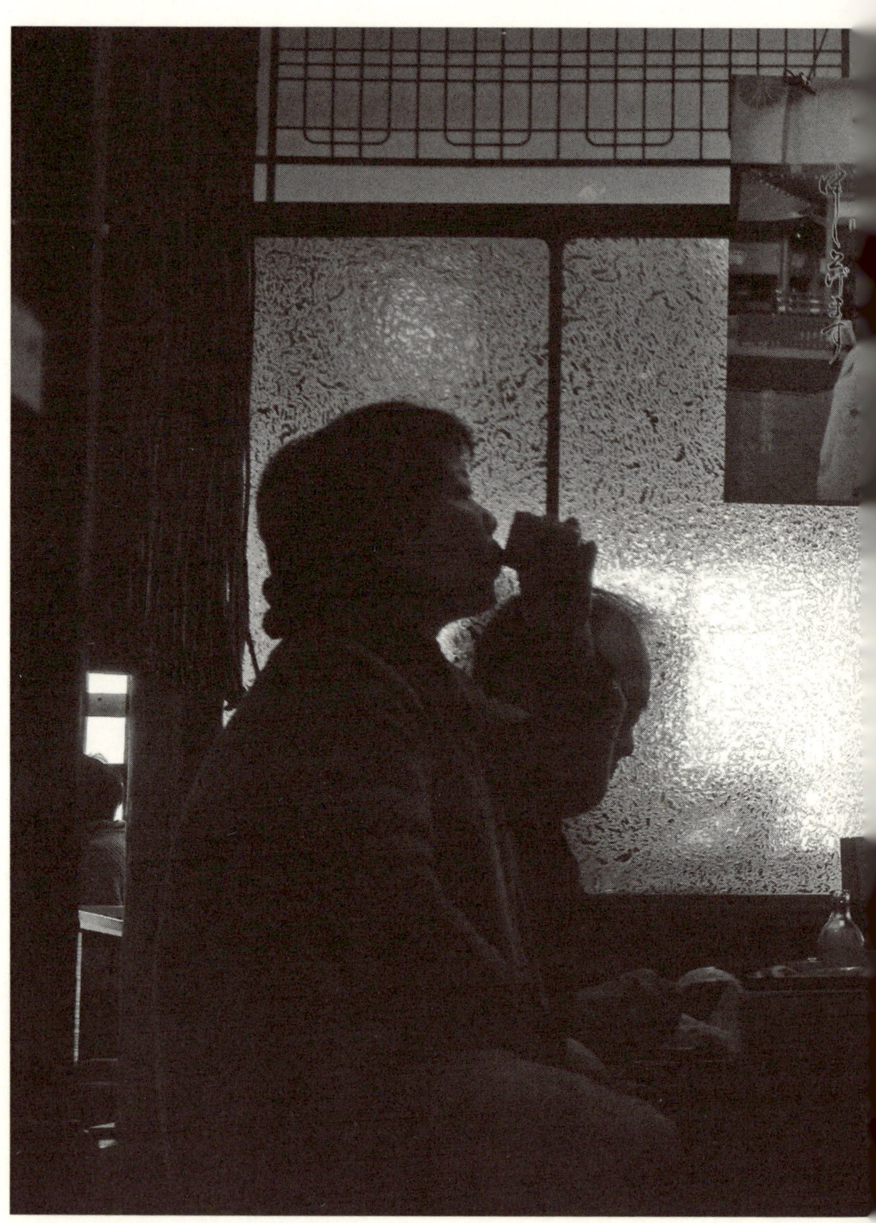

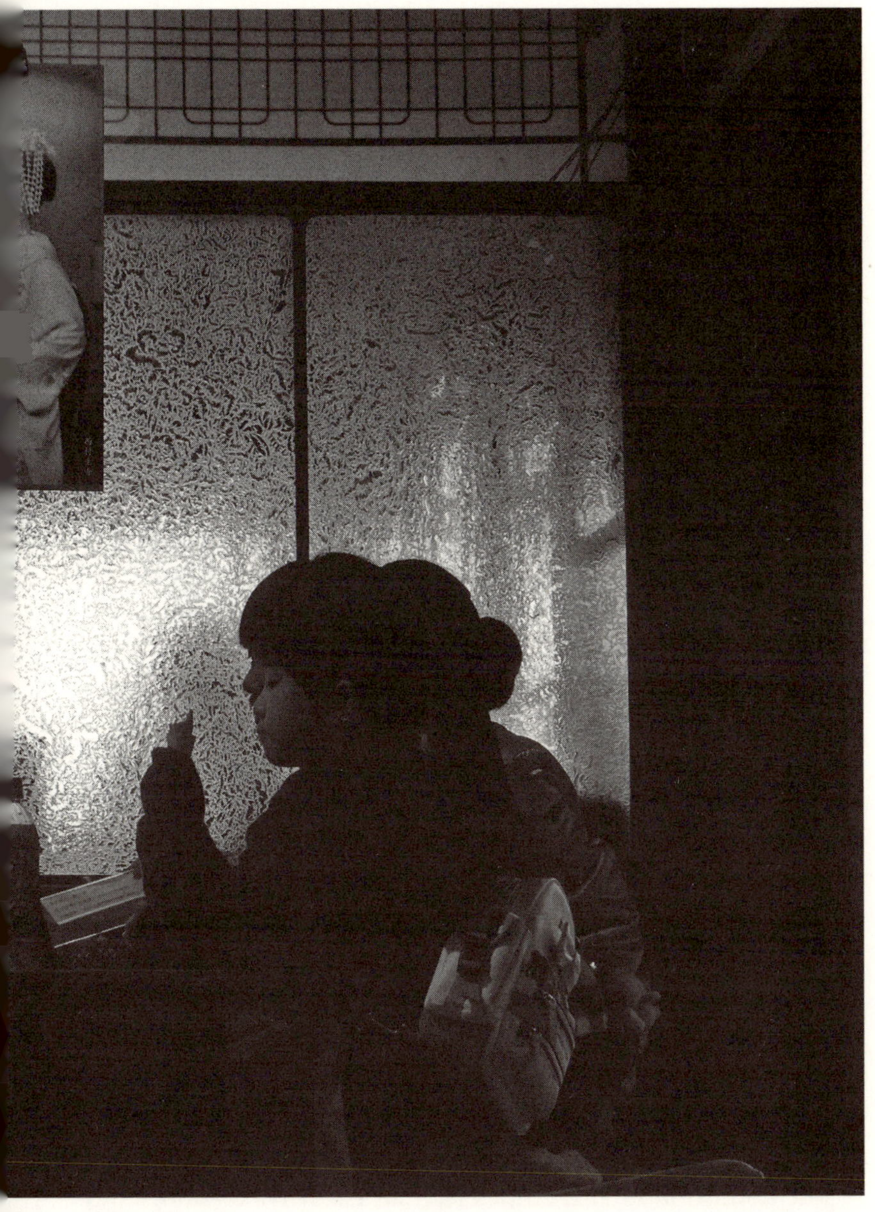

houses have moved in recent years from Osaka proper to the suburban Hanshin region, between Osaka and Kobe, these ceremonies are repeated every year. I have heard it said that Baron Fujita is most conservative in these matters.[45] I am told that the head housekeeper at the Baron's home until recently dressed her hair in the traditional style and wore a skirt with a train.

It is an interesting thing about the Hanshin: while the customs of the urban merchant townhouse persist there, as an extension of life in Osaka, you still also find the rural customs native to that area.

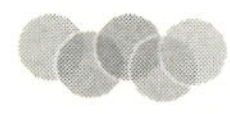

Old customs linger longest among artists and the demimonde. When I was in the third and fourth years of middle school, inspired by Miss Higuchi Ichiyō's story "Takekurabe," I longed for the neighborhood that centers on the Yoshiwara licensed quarter, and I would sneak out of the house to watch every event there as it came around—whether the Niwaka festival, or nighttime cherry-blossom viewing, or the procession of the *oiran*. But those sorts of events died out in Tokyo long before the great earthquake. Recently, in imitation of the Miyako-odori, the dance performance by apprentice geisha in Kyoto's Gion district, Tokyo began holding an event called Azuma-odori in Shinbashi, but of course it has not become as popular as the Gion performance. The reason is probably in part that not enough years have passed to make it an "event"; but it is also likely because in Tokyo, as in Osaka, there is no close relationship between ordinary townspeople and the demimonde. If it comes to that, the Miyako-odori and similar festivals are not solely events of the Gion. When the distinctive lanterns are hung at the corners of the cherry-tree-lined alleys, it is as if spring had come to all the neighborhoods of the old capital at once, and the whole populace grows merry. Similar *maiko* dance performances in Osaka—the Ashibe-odori, Naniwa-odori and so on—cannot compare with the Miyako-odori; nevertheless, they do serve to remind the people of the city that spring has arrived and to elicit a nostalgic affection for their hometown. At such times, citizens feel as though their neighborhood is part of a great family. Such events soften the hearts of the locals and immeasurably increase affection among them.

After all, the reason people say "Tokyoites have no hometown" is that the city's borders expand pointlessly, and familiarity is diluted across the whole city. Each of the cities of the Hanshin region has its own centers; in Osaka, for example, there is Senba, Nakanoshima and the neighborhood between Shinsaibashi and Dōtonbori; and, in Kyoto, the area from Shijō Kyōgoku to Gion Ishidanshita. But there is no such center in Toyko. If forced to identify one, we might name Ginza, or Shinjuku, or Kagurazaka, or Asakusa, but none of these coalesces into a definite center. Even the theater districts and red-light districts are scattered in all directions. This may be simply because Tokyo is such a large city,[46] but the lack of a center today, when a network of boulevards extends in every direction and inexpensive taxis can take you anywhere in twenty or thirty minutes, makes Tokyo like a family home without a dining room to gather in. Although Osaka has surpassed Tokyo in population and area since its expansion, the centers nevertheless remain where they have always been, and citizens still stream into them for sightseeing and shopping.

Festivals and other events tend to take place there all year round. The pleasure quarters there, too, are divided into Shinmachi, Horie, Nanchi and Kitashinchi, but they are concentrated in one area, about a mile in diameter, so they are all within easy walking distance. As a result, the sight of geisha strolling down the street and the festivities of the pleasure quarters become additional spectacles of the city at large, and even shop-boys, nursemaids, wives and daughters—people with no direct connection to the demimonde—look upon those women with affection.

That is why the annual events of that world are still celebrated eagerly in Osaka and, quite unsurprisingly, have come to be seen by citizens as seasonal outings that must not be allowed to fade away. How sad it would be for Osakans' calendars if, for example, the Hoekago festival held on the ninth day of the new year were to vanish. For myself, the mochi-pounding event held there at the end of the year has become particularly dear. The sight of the mochi being pounded as that great crowd of geisha sing year-end folk songs accompanied by shamisen—how it provokes in me a sense of the year's end! It is extremely regrettable that Osaka, which possesses such traditions, lacks a man of letters like Kubota Mantarō to record them. If even one such great novelist had lived in Osaka during the Meiji and Taishō eras, the city would have produced one or two works comparable to "Takekurabe" or *Sumidagawa*, but there is none.[47] This can safely be called a disgrace for such a large city. More broadly, it should be considered a loss to Japanese literature that all novelists discard their hometown and set their minds on Tokyo.

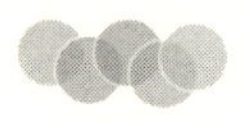

The fact that Osakans honor the old customs means they still hold an attachment to the legacy they inherited from their parents. I am totally ignorant of such matters, but, while the petit bourgeois class of Tokyo crumbles, buffeted wave after wave by the current of the times, the propertied middle class of Osaka still seems to hang on everywhere, firmly rooted. Walking the old and narrow streets of the Senba merchant quarter, one discovers how many small, privately run businesses are resisting the riptide of large-scale capitalism.

One sometimes meets old people in the Tokyo "low city" who fit the description of the so-called "failed Edokko." My own father was representative of the type: honest, fastidious, irritable, disinterested in fame or fortune, shy of strangers, reluctant to flatter, incompetent at getting on in the world, so that, working in trade, he simply could not contend with the pushiness of outsiders. In view of this, he was destined to fritter away the assets he inherited from his parents until, having reached old age, he became a burden to his children and relatives; but he never worried about that in the slightest. He grew almost smug as he approached insolvency and enjoyed his final years in an exceedingly carefree manner. That sort of old person is generally skinny, with strong legs that can walk several miles a day without trouble. Give them some pocket money, and they take it and stroll off toward Asakusa to while away half a day watching a movie and eating sushi at a street stall. They like sake, too, but prefer not to drink much of it; one cup with dinner leaves them tipsy. When drunk, they gossip happily and quickly fall into a peaceful slumber. An outsider might wonder what they are living for, but these old people are, themselves, naturally easygoing, so they don't

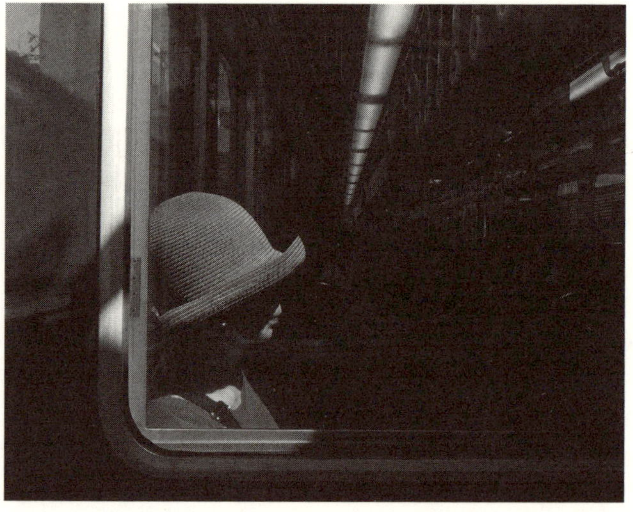

sulk about the state of the world or begrudge others their happiness. They meet even death—that of a family member and, of course, their own—without commotion, without lamentation, resigned to their destiny. On the other hand, they detest any dispute with relatives, any discord in the household, and try to remain aloof from it, maintaining harmony with everyone. Consequently, they present no hindrance to their children or relations, and never ask for anything that might cause a nuisance; to receive even the most trivial payment for anything causes them regret. Some work as custodians at elementary schools or ward offices, playing shogi or visiting the game parlor in their free time. At least one such old person is to be found in every household among the old families of Tokyo. They are especially numerous among my father's generation; among the younger generation, it's safe to say that Tsuji Jun is that type.[48] They might be dismissed as losers in the struggle for existence, and it's true that their failure was their own fault, because they were slackers who would not apply themselves; viewed from another perspective, however, there is a sense in which we must speak of them as we do of mountain hermits who travel into the city. When you meet one at this point in his life, whatever he may have been in the past, he gives the same impression of serenity as a Zen monk who has gained enlightenment. I have not met such a person since coming to Osaka. And when I ask friends here, they say that sort of character is exceedingly rare in Kansai.

They have a word here, *"yokuboke"* (greedy fool), that is not used in Tokyo. Which is to say that more common in Osaka is the type who, out of impatience to be making more and more money, find their eyes dazzled, their thoughts debased, and their character coarsened by greed, until at last they are shunned by society and left behind. In fact, Tokyoites cannot begin to imagine how Osakans fear the idea of being left penniless. Even if Tokyoites do not want to end up penniless themselves, they can make allowances for the mindset of the old men I mentioned above. Osakans, on the other hand, would not understand them at all. To Osakans, falling into such circumstances is simply too dreadful, and if on occasion they meet with such an old man, they shun him as a fool or a madman.

Those who have read French realist novels will likely know what great importance the French attach to property. Such great authors as Balzac, Flaubert and Zola never fail to describe the economic conditions of the characters in their works. Even in a romantic love story, when introducing the male or female protagonist, they explain that their father left a bequest of this much and their aunt a bequest of that much, and the interest earned on it annually amounts to this much, so they enjoy a monthly income of that much, and they have expenses of so much on this and so much on that, which leaves them with a surplus balance of this much—indeed, they write it all up most scrupulously. Some will go back three or four generations to explain in great detail the history of an inheritance, like the career of a household's fortunes: upon the death of Count so-and-so, who left a fortune of X thousand francs, just X thousand francs was bequeathed to Marquis so-and-so, and, when the Marquis died, he left X thousand francs, which fell into the hands of so-and-so. Osakans hold exactly the same idea of "property." The cadet houses will get this much when the main house's assets are divided; and with that as capital, they will do this much trade and invest this much in real estate and other property; this much will go to the eldest son, this much to the younger sons, and this much toward the daughter's marriage arrangements— it seems to be all that middle-class people think about.[49] As a result, Osakans possess, from childhood, a keen ability to calculate profit and loss and a surprisingly developed sensitivity to the topic of money, such that Tokyo middle-school boys and girls, by comparison, are perfect idiots on the same subject. The other day, one newspaper published an article quoting a clerk at some department store as saying that Tokyo housewives throw away their receipt at the register without even looking at it, while eighty or ninety percent of Osaka housewives carefully take theirs home, and I'm sure this is accurate.

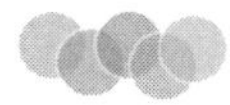

There is a passage in a letter written by Rai San'yō's widow, Rieko, in which she expresses gratitude to her husband for not neglecting to plan for her and their children after his death, so that they would never go hungry, even should the worst happen to him.[50] There is a certain moral fastidiousness among Tokyoites that, upon learning such a poet of patriotic righteousness had concerned himself with amassing wealth, causes them to think, "Ah, that's the Chinese influence," and to suddenly despise him. However, it cannot be acceptable, even for a loyalist poet, to abandon his wife and children on the roadside, so surely it is better for him to have made provisions. Certainly, high-minded poverty is no selling point for an artist these days. Moreover, since no one takes any pride in such poverty, we probably have a lot to learn from the Osaka attitude—and especially a dissolute fellow such as myself. At any rate, here in Osaka you are unlikely to meet the sort of artist who spends money like water when he has it and then, when it's gone, is suddenly so hard up that he cannot make it through the next day. In general, all the artists here, regardless of status, skill, or talent, whether of the first rank or the second, are wise to the ways of making money. It is therefore natural that, when one becomes a successful author, such considerations exert not the slightest negative influence on their work. In this regard, the late Mr. Koide Narashige was the most exemplary artist in Osaka.[51] He was just the sort of well-liked person, a witty conversationalist with a roguish side, who completely enchanted shrewd people with the childishly simplicity of his manner. At the same time, he had another side, employing a keen intellect in both his private life and in his literary production, such that one sometimes heard people say behind his back, "that Koide's cunning!" But considering that he left behind such an impressive oeuvre, one understands the true self of the artist that lies beneath the skin, apart from any "cunning" or "shrewdness." He possessed toward his work a ceaseless devotion and a passion that burned like fire. I think that, because he was a native Osakan and, what's more, born into a merchant family, he was equipped by birth with a genius for the life of his hometown. I do not mean thereby to imply any criticism. If it is part of the common sense of that region to live frugally and take care to make provisions for one's livelihood,[52] then it is hardly any wonder he possessed this same common sense. What's more, Koide held a deep affection for his region and never moved away, so such behavior was required of him as a matter of social etiquette. As for novelists and the like, wherever they happen to live, their audience is Tokyo journalists, who are easily dealt with. But painters—and particularly painters working in the Western style—absolutely must take care to get along with the people among whom they live. An easygoing person like me is completely ignorant of such things, but one savvy merchant told me "Koide is always on his guard," so I think there must have been something sharp and forceful in his dealings with such men, just as there was in his painting. At any rate, no one else so skillfully combined artistic talent with the Osakan character. I feel that is the true mark of an artist born of a locale.

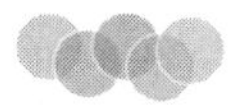

Among Osakan maxims is one that advises, "A Kyoto woman makes the best wife." It may be true that Kyoto women are better than Osakans at keeping house and cleverer at managing the budget, but, to my mind, most Osaka women are by no means inferior. I once employed two women from the prefectural vocational training school as secretaries. I say "secretaries," but since my work habits are highly irregular, the position was nothing like an office job; I had them live in the house with us, just like family, where they worked at most twenty days in a month and spent the other days just hanging around. It was not as physically restrictive as the work of an ordinary career woman. But what surprised me was that the two of them rarely left the house. They stayed at home whether or not there was anything that needed doing. Consequently, they had no opportunity to waste money. They wouldn't go out to the movies, or to a concert, or on a sightseeing excursion, unless we invited them at our own expense. Perhaps that was to be expected of girls of good family such as these, but it struck me as strange, used as I am to the disposition of young literary enthusiasts in Tokyo. First of all, no woman in Tokyo who was studying literature at a vocational train school, living in the household of a novelist, receiving something of a monthly salary, and enjoying some leisure besides, would ever be so meek. It's usual for young women of that age to go out to see friends if they have some free time—to dress up in smart Western clothes and hang about here or there—not to be always sitting at home. Whereas the young women I employed were so very compliant that they lacked the confidence or the drive to do such things. If you're wondering whether they sat at a desk all day studying—they did not. I don't possess a large personal library at home, but I have more books than the typical household, and I was ready to answer any questions, and besides, there were visitors to the house from the world of literature, yet these young women took no advantage of such opportunities and stimuli, apparently having lost all interest in literature as soon as they graduated. When I noticed how they did spend their time, it was in reading lowbrow women's magazines, helping the rest of the household with the chores, or doing some sewing; to all appearances, they were no different from maids. In short, they were fundamentally homebodies. Since there was no danger that they might put on airs with their learning or clash with the family, they settled into our home easily, but it might have been better had they possessed enough spirit to challenge us just a bit, as well as some ambition in the scholarly arts. I heard the following from one of them. An acquaintance had found a job as a teacher in the provinces after graduation and, when the day came to leave Osaka, a

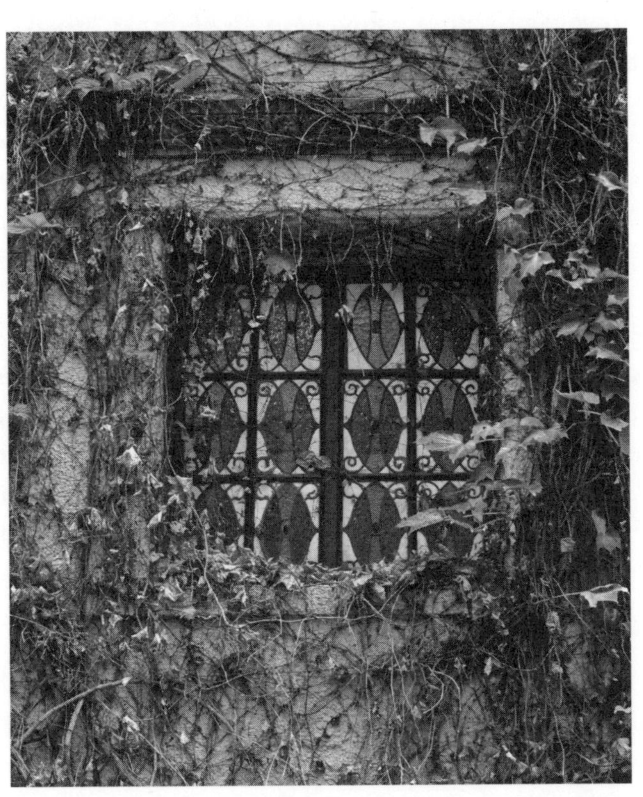

friend from the same class went to Umeda Station to see her off. Both the one that was leaving and the one that was seeing her off were so sad to be parting that they burst into tears. I could perhaps understand if she were heading to the far ends of Kyushu or Hokkaido, but she was going no farther than Tokyo! Isn't it the most touching story?

However, because young women of Osaka are like that, it's easy to imagine them, as wives, tender-hearted, gentle and skillful at running the household. Even the richest girl seems ready and able to take control of the management of household finances when she is married off to a businessman with only 100 yen. It is not unusual to find among them intelligent widows or wives who establish a trade and run a business themselves, supervising clerks and staff. And while it is not as common, there are among the mothers of my acquaintance two or three who, using money inherited from their deceased husband as capital, invest small sums here and there and support their children with the profits. In Tokyo, a woman speculator or moneylender is thought to be quite eccentric and immediately becomes a topic of gossip, but they're not considered unusual at all in Osaka.

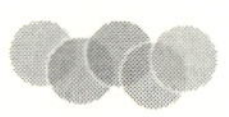

This is why life in a middle-class Osakan household is gloomy and sad in a way Tokyoites can hardly imagine. An Osaka friend of mine cursed the stinginess of people in Kyoto, saying "Even in the depths of winter, Kyoto people will stoke a fire no warmer than a firefly for their guests," but Osakans are just as frugal. Among the people I deal with in my everyday life are many who, though Osakan, aspire to fashionable society and so affect Tokyo ways, but they cannot really compare to Tokyoites due to their penny-pinching at home. First, if you live in some splendor in Osaka, people will shun your society, saying, "That family over there are Tokyo-style." Apparently, frugal Osakans set their household budgets much tighter than they can in fact afford. Moreover, what they call a splendid "Tokyo-style" household is nothing like the real Tokyo manner. If Tokyoites live in splendor, they do so in every aspect, without distinguishing between their public and private lives. Whereas here, though they may lead a splendid life in public, that comes to an end once they retreat to the private sphere, where no one can see them.

There are countless examples of the stinginess of the Keihan region, but I will cite only two I witnessed first-hand. Once, when I went to a certain restaurant to eat sukiyaki, the lady I was escorting took home one raw egg left over from our meal in the sleeve of her kimono. I could not help but be surprised, particularly since the lady was not the wife of some merchant but the hostess of one of the city's top teahouses. And then, what makes me uncomfortable in Osaka is when, waiting at night at the terminal station of the Hankyu or Hanshin line, one sees businessmen come along, take the evening newspaper they've finished reading out of their pocket and thrust it at the boy in the newsstand. The boy then takes the paper and exchanges it for a different evening paper, which the businessman quickly shoves in his pocket as he walks away. A Tokyoite would probably have no idea what was going on, but it goes without saying that the *Osaka Asahi* and the *Osaka Mainichi* are the most widely-read evening newspapers in Osaka and, as a result, the papers that sell out the fastest, while the other evening papers usually do not sell out and

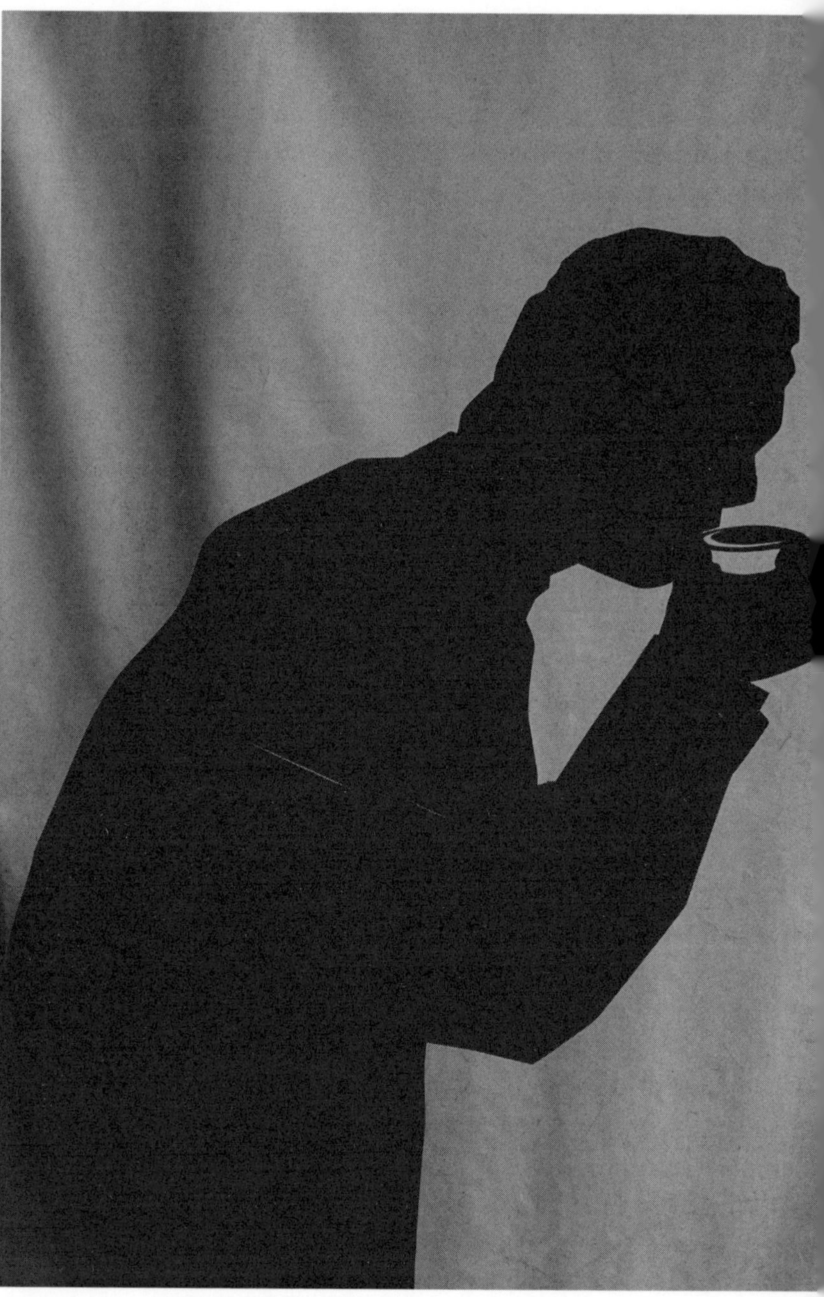

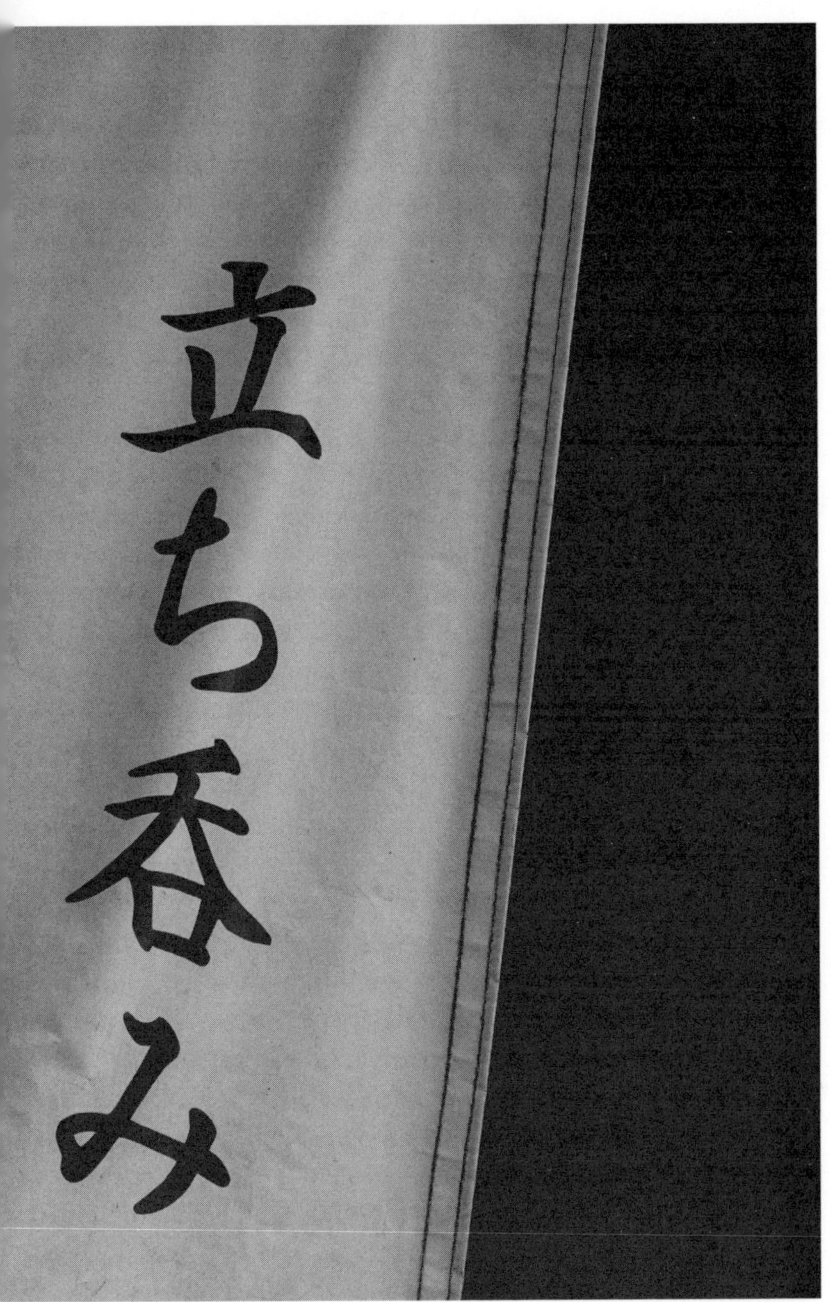
立ち呑み

are discounted—three copies for 3 or 5 *sen*—as the evening wears on. (The *Osaka Mainichi* sells out faster than the *Osaka Asahi.* There is considerable cunning involved in the selling of evening papers, too. There are some sellers who, if you ask for "The *Asahi* and the *Mainichi,*" will place one of those on top but hide some other newspaper underneath and hand it to you.) So then, if you get the *Osaka Asahi* or the *Osaka Mainichi,* you read through it quickly (it is essential, however, that you handle it carefully, without getting it too wrinkled), and then, when you give it to the newsboy, he will happily exchange it for a different paper. In other words, for the price of two evening newspapers—the *Asahi* and the *Mainichi*—you can read four! In fact, there is a spectacle you can see much more frequently in the Kamitsutsui terminal station, in Kobe: a man who has just come out of the station gate quickly presents his newspaper; the newsboy, apparently understanding, quickly presents another. They both look a little embarrassed, but this exchange occurs efficiently every evening, almost as though the two had made a contract between themselves.

And then, when you peek inside the home, you discover that this frugality extends to the brightness of the electric lighting, the dining table and so on. In Tokyo, it is usual to make enough of each dish to have some leftovers, but in Osaka, they make just a little less than enough for the number of people, precisely. Come to think of it, the reason the so-called "Chōshū" cast-iron bathtub is so common in Kansai is probably because it saves on the cost of fuel. Those tubs seem truly inconvenient to anyone who grew up with the kind of wooden bathtub common in Tokyo; my family too, felt defeated by it when we first moved here.

However, speaking from an economic standpoint, we can heat it using all the rubbish that would have gone to the ragman; and it heats up quickly, so once you have one in your home, you find there's nothing else so convenient. If it's big enough, you won't scald yourself by leaning against the sides, and so I've lately come to prefer this primitive sort of bathtub.

Speaking of bathtubs, Osaka merchants, like their Tokyo counterparts, generally used to go to a public bathhouse rather than heat water at home. And then, housewives would go only once every five days or so and spend one or two hours there scrubbing themselves thoroughly. Considered from that perspective, there may be an economic reason why the inside of an Osakan home seems unsanitary to someone from Tokyo. It is true that, as everyone knows, traditional Kyoto townhouses have a triangular box placed in the toilet,[53] but the kitchen, bath and toilet in an Osaka house are just as filthy. Some of the Western-style houses in the Hanshinkan are equipped with flush toilets, but they are so dirty you wonder what the point is. Edokko pride themselves on the fact that, even if they're dressed in rags, their underwear and footwear, at least, are fresh; having seen the bathrooms of Osakans, I can only suppose that their undergarments are unclean, too. While I'm on the subject, people in Kansai are not nearly as fussy as Edokko about their *tabi* socks. The fact that they are always wearing saggy *tabi* is not due simply to indifference; it comes rather from the economic consideration that *tabi* do not last very long. This would never occur to an unobservant Tokyoite; I first learned about it after asking a geisha in Kyoto.

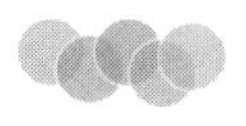

Once, I was enjoying myself at a teahouse in Kyoto's Gion quarter when, as it got late, I suddenly felt hungry and asked the five or six geisha in the room, "Won't you eat something?" They were long-time acquaintances who did not stand on ceremony, and, as I asked each one in turn, "How about you?" "And you?" they all shook their head and said, "I don't need anything," since they had already eaten somewhere before joining me. As I reached the last and youngest one, though, she thought a moment and said bashfully, "I can't say anymore," and laughed. It seems this girl was the only one in the group who was hungry. But for a Tokyo geisha in such a situation to say "I can't say anymore" would be inexcusable. I'm no longer knowledgeable about such things now that I've become utterly provincial, but I think that, in Tokyo, she would begin and end with some apologetic phrase, or else would say, frankly, "Thank you, I think I will." Somehow, simply smirking and mumbling, "I can't say anymore" seems very "Kamigata." Not only the geisha in Kansai but the married women, too, express their feelings in rather few words, and euphemistically. Compared to the Tokyo manner, it sounds sophisticated and extremely alluring. What is more, since those words come softly, in that wet, cloying voice I mentioned above, they are all the more charming and suggestive.

Because the Tokyo dialect has today become the standard language, it is grammatically the most exact, expressively the finest and freest, and the most convenient for explaining something in exhaustive detail, but as a language for an elegant Japanese woman of the classical type, it is totally unsuitable. First of all, Tokyo dialect makes it all too easy to speak too much. Of course, there are talkative women in the Kamigata region too, but the effect they have is different from their Tokyo counterparts because the language is different. For example, people in Osaka use post-positions less frequently and are less fussy when they do use them. This may not be the most accurate example, but in Tokyo dialect, *atashi <u>wa</u> wakaranai wa* ("I don't know") and *atashi <u>de wa</u> wakaranai wa* (more humbly, "I don't know [though others might]") are used in different circumstances. In Osaka, however, no such distinction is made. In either case, they would probably say, *uchi wakarehen.*[54] If I find that this example is incorrect, I will revise it, but the overall point I am trying to make stands. Osaka dialect is oddly coarse in this aspect, as I first discovered when I was writing the novel *Manji* (*Quicksand*, 1928–30) in the voice of an Osaka woman.[55] I started to write the novel in Tokyo dialect; then, when I went to rewrite it in Osaka dialect I found that there were some things that could be expressed only in one dialect and not in the other. (By the way, recent novels often eliminate post-positions even in Tokyo dialect. Perhaps it is the Kamigata influence, but a true Tokyoite would never speak in such a manner. Tokyoites are rather the type to draw out the post-position. Even if it might sound as though they are abbreviating it, they're absolutely mouthing the post-position.) Osakans also omit the "*to*" post-position after a quotation. When they mean to say '*Nani nani*' *to osshaimashita* ("He said 'such and such'"), they instead say '*Nani nani*' *iyaharimashiten.*[56] '*Tanizaki*' *to iu hito* ("A person called 'Tanizaki'") becomes '*Tanizaki*' *iu hito*. Furthermore, the distinctions drawn in Tokyo dialect with the various expressions for "in that case" generally get lumped together into one expression in Osaka dialect. And, as these examples suggest, Osaka

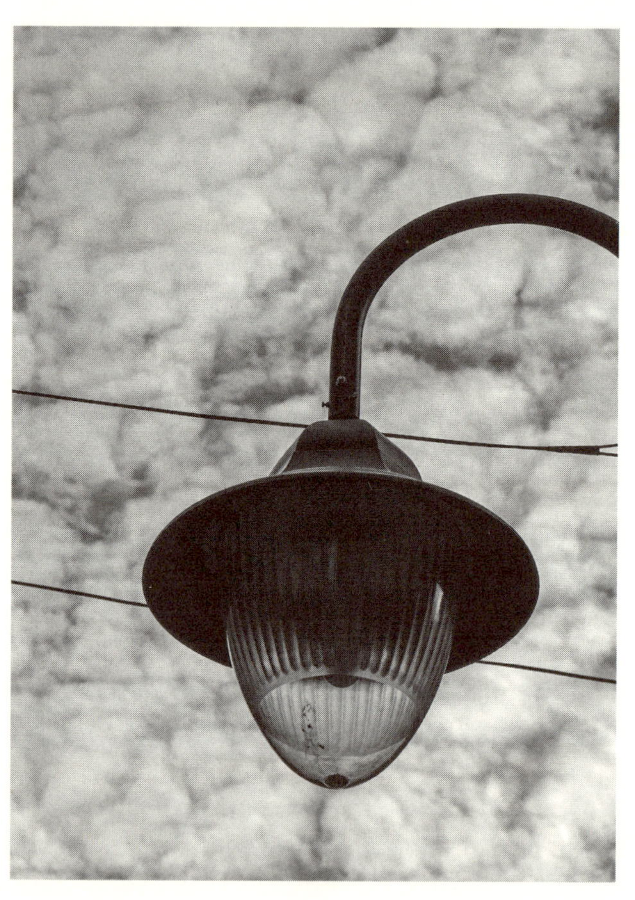

dialect has very few polite or honorific forms. This might seem rather surprising for the Kamigata region, but it's true. Tokyo, starting with *asobase* style, is truly rich in forms showing degrees of respect and complex variations in occupation, age, social class and so on. Take *suru* ("to do"), for example; off the top of my head, I can think of at least nineteen variations, each with a slightly different feeling. The Osaka dialect has nowhere near so many. Tokyo uses the honorific prefix *o-* more often, too. Osaka schoolgirls never say *o-tomodachi* ("friend"), but simply *tomodachi.* Such refined usage is seldom heard here. As a result, in the Osaka dialect, there are intervals between words in which the listener infers the sentiment of the speaker, and it does not do to express everything in the finest detail, right down to the subtlest emotional nuances, as Tokyo dialect does. Tokyoites talk in a constant stream, without pause, whereas in Osaka, even if someone speaks at length, little gaps open up here and there. In terms of functionality, Tokyo dialect is clearly superior, and, when it comes to expressing the thoughts and feelings of contemporary people, nothing else serves the purpose. Nevertheless, there is something vulgar in the way it leaves nothing unexpressed, exposing every nook and cranny. That is why, when people speaking Tokyo dialect use excessively polite, roundabout phraseology, they sound on the contrary unrefined. In other words, because, in their complete mastery, they will go on and on, they end up being manipulated by language. Here in the East where silence is considered a virtue, language, too, is made to suit the national character, so if it is developed in contradiction to that virtue, its beauty, at the very least, will be lost. In the language of the women of the Kansai region, there survives the distinction of the Japanese of long ago: to speak only a third of what one wants to convey, while leaving the remainder vaguely implied. This may no longer be the case among the general public, but it is comforting to know that such beauty is still being handed down by some.

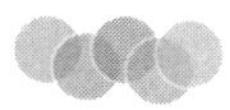

Even when it comes to indecent conversation, Kamigata women understand the art of conducting it in a dignified and suggestive way. Done in Tokyo dialect, it inevitably becomes lewd, so married women of good family never engage in such conversation; but the same is not necessarily the case here, where even amateurs at that sort of thing can carry on such a conversation without lowering themselves. And because they are amateurs, it is strangely all the more seductive to hear. In fiscal matters, too, they state their desires quite skillfully. Ostentatious Tokyoites ask for trouble by saying things they don't really believe, whereas in Osaka, the character of the place being what it is, a softer mode of expression has naturally developed—less vulgar, one that avoids angering people and at the same time doesn't hurt the wallet—since the dialect has suited itself to the city's characteristic indirectness, which sounds almost like playing dumb. The story is often repeated that Osakans, when they meet in the street, don't greet each other in the usual way but instead say, "Are you making any money?" and, in fact, that turns out to be true at least among some men, but women never use that expression. While they may be silently calculating profit and loss in their heads, they never discuss it openly. And yet, it is amazing how they manage to accomplish their goals in the end without forgetting their manners at any point, whether attacking or defending, by using a mode of expression so roundabout as to seem like a riddle. They can do this while demanding or denying a loan or conducting other such unseemly or brazen business; or letting you know of their poverty without saying as much; or implying selfishness without embarrassing the other person; or denying as though to affirm; or stating the hypothesis while leaving the conclusion unspoken. This is only possible between Osakans, though. If one party to the conversation is from Tokyo, he or she will either make the riddle so obscure that it is misunderstood or pretend not to understand, and one or the other will end up angry. Even I often realize after the fact that this has happened and grow either angry or regretful. Tokyoites must always remember this when keeping company with Osakans and must not take their words literally when discussing financial matters. For example, when you are giving someone a cash gift, even if they decline it so strenuously that you must forcibly stuff it into their pocket, that doesn't mean they don't want it. It is accepted practice here to give and receive gifts in this manner. (In Tokyo these days, we follow the style of students and exchange cash gifts without using gift envelopes, but here their use is not limited to cash gifts. And when women exchange cash, be it is a little as a single one-yen bill, they at least wrap it in a piece of special paper; even those on the most familiar terms do not offer each other naked cash.) Despite this, Tokyoites approach Osakans to borrow money and then, never receiving a definite answer no matter how much time passes, they go home angry. However, the Osakan certainly intended to imply a clear "yes" or "no" during the conversation. Their implication would indisputably qualify as a definite answer among fellow Osakans, but Tokyoites can't solve the riddle because they are used to speaking frankly. I think this sort of thing contributes greatly to Osakans' reputation among Tokyoites for cunning. It is not that they are cunning; that way of interacting is simply good manners in Osaka. As for Osakans, they make every effort to state their intentions, so as not to sound discourteous and anger short-tempered Tokyoites. However, I would like to offer some advice to them, too; and that is to express things more simply when talking to Tokyoites. If you do not, before you know it, you will come to be scorned and despised. Osaka women are generally amiable and charming, so it certainly comes from the very best intentions, but they truly do use the most toe-curling flattery. Many Tokyoites are bashful and become embarrassed when addressed too glibly; they take no pleasure in such conversation. Moreover, a contempt for the person who uses such flattery gets fixed in their mind. However, in Osaka, you meet many women of this type and realize that most of them are good, honest people.

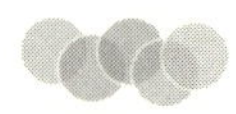

"Coming from Tokyo, Osaka is the only other place that really feels like a metropolis": this is another saying of Nagano Sōfū's, and, come to think of it, although Kyoto is a big city, it doesn't feel that way because the people's sense of humor is rather dull,[57] whereas Osakans are very sharp. On that count, certainly, they are metropolitans, and neither men nor women in Osaka are inferior to Tokyoites in their sense for jokes and banter. As for comic storytelling and the like, in Tokyo, light jokes predominate, sometimes with a hint of irony, whereas here, the stories progress

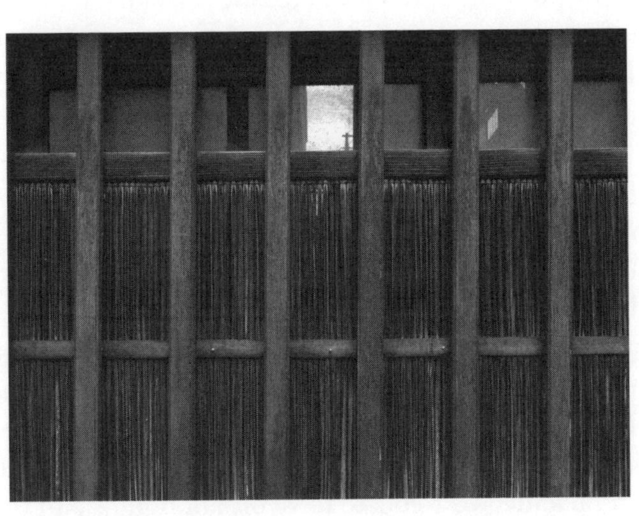

slowly and rather gravely, building to a ridiculousness beyond words. That ambiguous way of speaking, as if playing dumb, in itself sounds funny to Tokyoites, even if the subject is serious. I still recall when I had just arrived here and went to see a comedy movie, listening to the *benshi* narrator, even the most trivial thing he said was so funny I almost died laughing.[58] However, in addition to the comicality inherent in the words themselves, a sense of comedy has developed among the audience. Edokko are not the only people who understand jokes; Osakans do, too. And this development becomes clear when you compare them to the people of more rural areas to the West, such as Chugoku and the island of Shikoku.

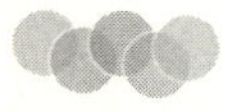

When people in Tokyo think of acquiring a second home in the Kamigata region, they all set their sights on the Saga neighborhood of Kyoto. When they move there, though, they quickly discover that it is surprisingly unpleasant, both in the climate and in the character of the local people. Sadanji told me some time ago that the late Takata Minoru, having decided to relocate to Kyoto, bought a plot of land in the village of Kinugasa, just north of the city, and had a house built there, but lost all patience after just a month and fled back to Tokyo.[59] Kyoto is penetratingly cold in the winter and dreadfully hot in the summer, although spring and fall are spectacular. But even if they can put up with the climate, ordinary people don't settle down in Kyoto for long (excepting such people as Mr. Saionji and Mr. Kiyoura).[60] There are many aspects of life there that tend to infuriate Tokyoites, such as the character of the local tradesmen and the disposition of the neighbors, and it's impossible to make the kind of close friends with whom you can let down your guard. It was probably this sort of thing that caused Master Kōda to flee, as well.[61]

That reminds me: I was in the mountains of Hakone when the 1923 earthquake struck. Since the mountain road to Tokyo was blocked by a landslide, I boarded an express train at Numazu on September 4, bound for Osaka. My intention was to travel to Kobe and board a ship there back to Yokohama, but no one was allowed to board without a special temporary permit, so I spent three or four days moving between Kyoto, Osaka and Kobe. Swarms of citizens had gathered outside Umeda, Sannomiya and Kobe stations to meet refugees from the earthquake and to distribute care packages to those of us lined up at the exits. Spaces for our entertainment had been set up in front of the railway station, and the activity at Umeda Station was especially remarkable, but what really surprised me was that the plaza in front of Shichijo Station in Kyoto was quiet, no different from a regular weekday. Seeing that truly gave me a strange feeling. Nothing since has so vividly illustrated the local character of Kyoto. Around that time, a rumor spread that I was relocating to the Kamigata region, and the mistress of a teahouse in the Gion quarter said to me, "If that happens, and then great crowds of important people follow you to Kyoto, what will become of us locals?"; that was the candid attitude of Kyotoites. While the people seemed happy to find their city becoming a sort of capital again, there was a sense that, "If a lot of high-ranking people immigrate to the city en masse, who knows what will happen to us," or, "It's better if those people just stay away"—in short, a stubbornly passive attitude of self-preservation. Therefore, rather than willingly console victims, they focused on re-fraining from any extravagant indulgence and, in a spirit of self-restraint, behaved so as not to be scolded by the police or criticized by the newspapers. That is why the streets of Kyoto were less lively than usual and why the people, having quickly locked their doors in fear of groundless rumors, fell dead silent, as if forming a vigilante group rather than organizing relief for strangers. Meanwhile, relief efforts were thriving in Osaka, and people in towns like Ashiya along the Hanshin Railway main line were in a cheerful mood, listening calmly, as usual, to their phonographs.

Kyoto might seem to better suit the nature of my work, but that was not in fact the case. So long as I can remain detached from the business world, with which I have no connection, it seems best to live in Osaka. I have never lived in the center of the city, but I think I could live even there, as long as the atmosphere suited me. It is said that people there are greedy and vulgar about money, but Osaka is a merchant city, and isn't it natural for merchants to be greedy?[62] The only difference from Kyoto is that, here, people are openly greedy—and isn't that a good thing? I was a bit nauseated at first, because the local character was so different from Tokyo, but, as I became accustomed to it, in due course I discovered things to love amid the greed. It feels straightforward—more expansive, more manly, simply more impressive than the pallid intellectual class of Tokyo.

Two or three years ago, the great artist Kiyokata, who had never visited the Kamigata region due to his hatred of trains, traveled down the Tōkaidō highway for the first time in his life, in a car.[63] According to his memoir from that time, Kiyokata stopped on the way to do some sightseeing in Nagoya and found the atmosphere extremely interesting. His guide on the highway had thought he probably should not take Kiyokata to unremarkable downtown neighborhoods and had avoided such places, but the downtown unexpectedly drew the master's eye and piqued his interest. Reading that, I thought, "Yes, that's just how it would be." It may have been natural for the guide to think that someone from Tokyo wouldn't be interested in seeing the downtown, but as for me, although I don't know about Nagoya, when I walk the side streets in the cities of Kansai, I feel deeply nostalgic, recalling my childhood years. Every trace of the past has disappeared from the "low city" of today's Tokyo,[64] and yet, in the old neighborhoods of Kyoto and Osaka, you still find, unexpectedly, houses that somehow resemble the old earthen storehouses and rowhouses, with their latticework fronts. Ever since what happened to Yokohama, next-door to Tokyo, there's not a single big city that *feels like* a big city. The places that called to mind the streetscapes of old Japan are all gone, it's safe to say. However, if you go to the area around Muromachi in Kyoto, or Tanimachi, Kōzu, or Shitaderamachi in Osaka, you think to yourself, "Ah, this is what Tokyo used to look like," and you feel as though you'd found your forgotten hometown. In fact, Tokyo, too, used to be full of such deep, narrow townhouses, with dirt-floored passageways running all the way back. My home in Kayabachō was just such a house. In the summers, we would set out a bamboo bench for passersby and sit up late, talking with our neighbors or playing shogi. Here in Kansai, that sort of relaxed atmosphere survives, even in a great city like Osaka. The side streets of the

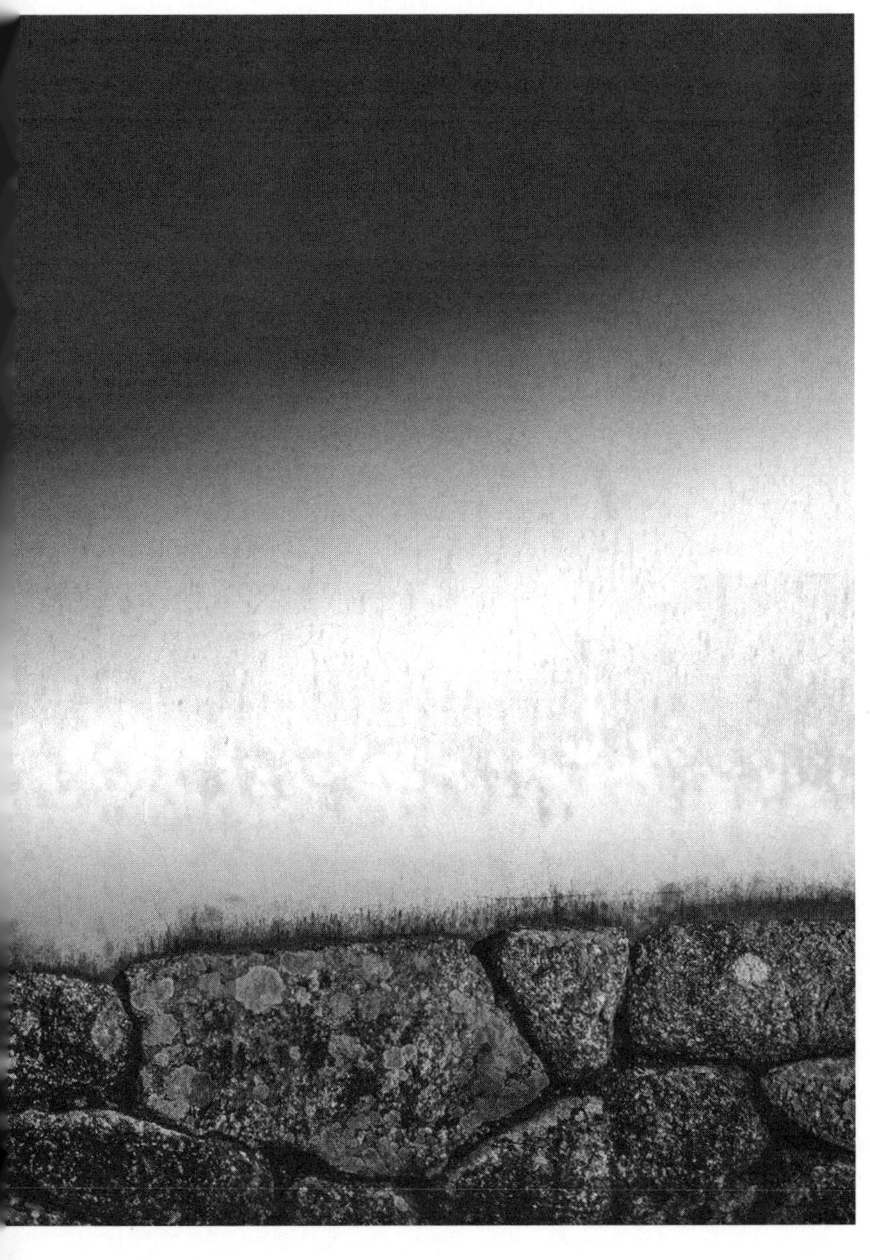

bustling metropolis are lined with trim, cozy little houses, and through the open lattice shutters one catches glimpses of back-alley life—in the six-mat front room, with the pillars and the floorboards polished to a shine, stands a long hibachi; the master of the house, in a quilted jacket, prepares a stew with his spirited wife. In the past, merchants and artisans all lived in such places, and there are still many to be found in the downtown districts of Senba and Shimanouchi. Kansai is gradually erecting great tall buildings in imitation of Tokyo, but only along the main boulevards, so the sight of those back-alley neighborhoods will probably, surprisingly, survive, as long as the city is never burnt to the ground.[65] Apparently, the Pontochō neighborhood is not to be rebuilt by Kyoto if it burns down again, but it has not yet gone to ruin, I'm happy to say.

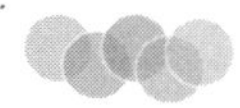

Living in Kansai for some time now, I have become familiar with various local conventions, manners and customs, as explained above, and when I go to watch the Bunraku puppet theater now, it makes an impression on me completely different from when I watched it in the past with the eyes of a Tokyoite. Certainly, the attitude of present-day Osakans toward the puppet theater is different from that of Tokyoites to the Mokuami Kabuki theater there.[66] Tokyoites watching the social milieu of the shogunate and the early Meiji era as represented in Kabuki feel it to be a part of the classical world, one or two ages removed from the present. But I dare say this is not the case for Osakans watching the puppet theater. They sense that there is, within those plays, something close to their own surroundings and everyday emotions, and this strike a chord with them, wrings tears of sympathy from them, and arouses a sense of unspeakable nostalgia. At least Osakans in their forties and fifties, watching those plays, recall their childhood and lose themselves in fond memories. And this effect is not limited to the domestic plays *Meido no hikyaku* (*Courier for Hell*) and *Shinjū ten no Amijima* (*The Love Suicides at Amijima*);[67] from the beginning, Jōruri dramas have been written to the standards of the general public, and even the large-scale historical plays feature themes and settings familiar to ordinary people and thereby try to play upon their true feelings. Even today, the theater in the conservative Kamigata region still possesses the power to move the merchant class and the common folk. Take the scene in *Chūshingura* (*The Treasury of the Loyal Retainers*), for example, where Kanpei commits ritual suicide: I used to hate that part when I saw it performed on the Tokyo Kabuki stage—as the wrinkled old lady entered from beyond the hanging curtain of the lantern-shaped stage entrance—it seemed to me rather drab.[68] It was not until I became familiar with the puppet theater here that I at last understood the attitude, the objective of those playwrights who unfailingly include such scenes in every period drama. In fact, that sort of scene is a realistic depiction of life in the countryside around here. And if you go out toward Yamazaki even now, you can see old farmhouses in the tall grass that are little changed from the time in which those plays are set. There are shabby thatched roofs all around, under which Yoichibei himself might have lived, and is not unusual to encounter old women just like O-Kaya in both aspect and manner of speech, and young women like O-Karu.[69] Umegawa and Chūbei's village of

Ninokuchimura, Sawaichi's Tsubosaka Temple, the village with the sushi shop in *Yoshitsune senbonzakura* (*Yoshitsune and the Thousand Cherry Trees*)—all these villages and towns still exist just as they did in the plays, and you can catch sight of people there who bear a striking resemblance to Magoemon, or Sawaichi, or Gonta, or O-Sato.[70] Once you are here, you can truly comprehend the significance of the puppet theater as a local art form. This is not so readily apparent simply from listening to the reciters; what's truly astonishing are the puppets' faces. Those that at first seem grotesque, when I stare at them intently, suddenly call to mind some local person I meet in my daily life. The faces of the old woman puppets are especially good. The face of O-Kaya, for instance, the adoptive mother in *Meido no hikyaku*—such faces still exist in the city streets today. And then, old men like Magoemon and Sōgan, merchants like Hachiemon, young husbands like Jihei—all are to be found among one's circle of acquaintance.[71] The faces of the young-woman puppets, too, truly capture a certain sensation, though seemingly made without special effort. If you look carefully, all of them—of course the women of the pleasure and merchant quarters such as Umegawa and O-San, but also the shogun's wives and princesses like Wakaba no naishi and Princess Yaegaki—have the faces of Osaka ladies.[72] Those puppet faces lurk beneath the features of the smart young wives and daughters who live along the Hanshin main line.

How utterly divorced from everyday life seems the very same *michiyuki* scene of O-Kara and Kampei in *Chūshingura* when it has been "Edo-ized" for the Kabuki stage. Seeing it, one understands how much more deeply rooted is the Osaka puppet theater. Furthermore, Kabuki is now performed almost exclusively in Tokyo, whereas the puppet theater is not limited to the Osaka Bunraku. It is performed at various other theaters, first among which is the Gennojō troupe on Awaji Island; the puppet theater spread west from Osaka and crossed over to Awaji Island and to Shikoku, where it has become intimately linked to the farming community.

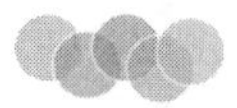

I think, in the above, I've touched on every matter that I intended to discuss, so I will set down my pen here. Regarding the food of Kansai, I've written before for various magazines; there's nothing new to say about it, now that Tokyo has been completely conquered by Osaka cuisine. And this region's advantages of warm climate and infrequency of great fires, earthquakes and other such calamities go without saying. The primer I used in elementary school taught me that "Our great empire of Japan is a land of temperate climate and scenic beauty ..." but, living in Tokyo, I did not at all feel it to be so; rather the opposite. Only after coming here could I accept that the book's lesson was not simply national pride but the truth. If we are to locate the "Japan" to which that statement applies, it must be the western half of the main island, from Osaka to the Chūgoku region. This is Japan's geographical heart, a region open to foreigners from ancient times and known to them, which came, perhaps naturally, to represent Japan. Honestly, from that perspective, it seems that Kansai is the metropole, and Kanto the provinces. Settsu, Kawachi and Izumi provinces are fine, too. The further west you go from there, the paler the earth, the warmer the climate, the

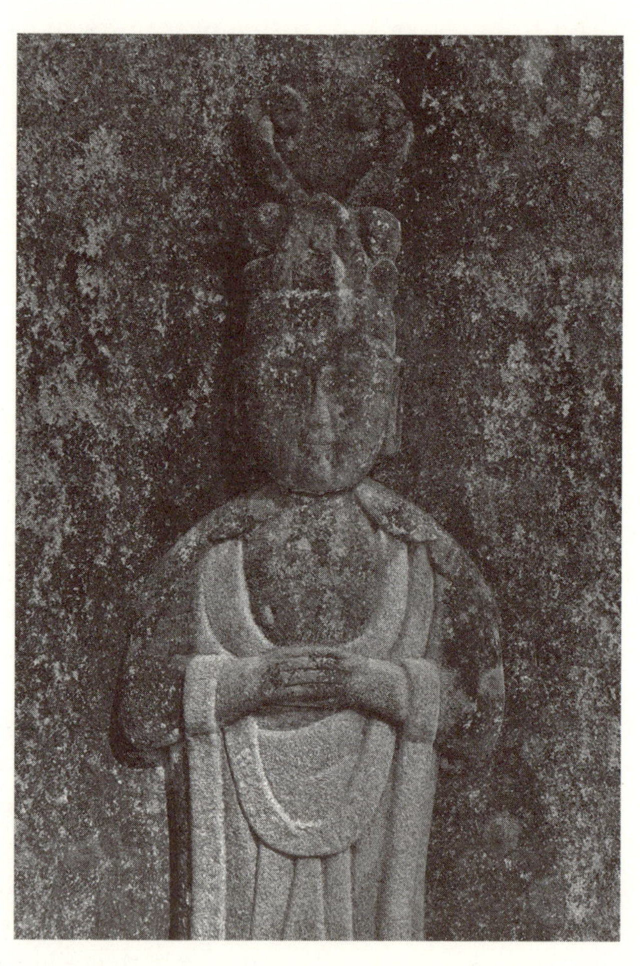

sweeter the fish and the more vivid the scenery.[73]

Nevertheless, in the preceding, I have fully demonstrated that I by no means intend to praise this region unconditionally. When all's said and done, this is a fine place for new graduates looking to make their way in society, or for those who have already made a professional name for themselves, but it is not a place to raise children. Tokyo is the only place to raise a boy—and certainly a girl—properly. It may reflect a more general change in the nature of students since my own time, but I'm sorry to say that students here lack self-confidence and adventurousness; instead, they possess the slickness of the shop clerk. They stand to inherit some property—however small—from their parents, and the climate is mild, and the food is cheap and delicious, so everyone is content with such small success and cherishes no greater ambition. It is not too bad in Osaka, but among the young people in the prosperous smaller cities of the Chūgoku region to the west are a great many who indulge in clever, petty argumentation while shutting their eyes to the broader situation. To be so rich in natural advantages is both a blessing and a curse.

Endnotes

1. Dōtonbori is a nightlife district in Osaka. Hōzenji yokochō is a narrow alley bordering it. Osaka investors established cafés in Tokyo after the earthquake, more like cabarets than the "pure cafés" Tokyoites were used to. Tsurugen seems to have been a tempura shop.
2. "Edokko" means "child of Edo," using the old name for Tokyo.

3. Twin brothers Shirai Matsujirō (1877–1951) and Ōtani Takejirō (1877–1969) co-founded the entertainment company that came to be known as the Shochiku Corporation. They began by managing Kabuki theaters before expanding into other fields, notably cinema. Shochiku assumed control of Tokyo's Kabuki-za in 1914.

4. Presumably Ichikawa Sadanji II (1880–1940) and Ōnoe Kikugorō VI (1885–1949), giants of the Kabuki stage.

5. Shiga Naoya (1883–1971), highly influential author of autobiographical fiction.

6. [JT] In addition to these, two of my *senpai* have been settled in Osaka for a long time: Kikuchi Yūhō (1870–1947), originally from Ibaraki prefecture, and Satō Kōroku (1874–1949), originally from Aomori prefecture.

7. Kusuyama Masao (1884–1950), writer and publisher. Osanai Kaoru (1881–1928), playwright, director and actor.

8. "Hanshin kenbunroku" (1925); see p. 15 of this volume for the English translation of the essay.

9. [JT] Of course, Kansai cuisine is generally superior both in ingredients and cooking methods, with the exception that the pure soy sauce used on sashimi and pickled vegetables is inferior to that of the Kanto region. The Kanto brands Kikkoman and Yamasa are sold here too, but I believe the quality is different.

10. *Zēroku* was a term of derision for the people of the Kamigata region.

11. [JT] To be precise: I sailed with my family from Shinagawa, in Tokyo, on the ship *Shanghai* around September 20, 1923, disembarking at Kobe. I then stayed briefly at the home of a friend in Ashiya. In early October we moved to a ridge near the Tōji-in temple, in Kyoto. We then rented a place in the temple precincts of Yōbōji, in Kyoto's Higashiyama Sanjō area, but, unable to endure the cold weather, we relocated to Kurakuen, between Osaka and Kobe, soon after the New Year and then set up our household in Okamoto that March. We have changed addresses from time to time since then but have never strayed from the Hanshin region.

12. The all-female Takarazuka Revue was established in 1913 at one terminus of the Hankyu Railway.

13. [JT] It is said that the Takarazuka Revue chooses stage-names for its actresses from phrases in the anthology *Hyakunin isshu* (*One Hundred Poets, One Poem Each*). Even so, they certainly find a great many ostentatious ones. I believe I even saw one actress named Ōzora Hiromi. [MPC] The names are archly poetic, artificially archaic—in a word, campy.
14. The Misaki-za theater, established in Tokyo in 1891, became well known for hosting female Kabuki troupes; in conventional Kabuki, all roles are performed by men.
15. Kishida Tatsuya (1892–1944) was director of the Takarazuka Opera Company.
16. Hakama are wide-legged trousers that were worn by schoolgirls in Tanizaki's time.
17. *Geta* and *zōri* are types of sandal worn with kimono.
18. Dolls representing an imperial court are displayed in homes on March 3.
19. Utagawa Kunisada (1786–1865), ukiyo-e artist.
20. Nagano Sōfū (1885–1949), artist of Japanese-style painting.
21. Specifically, the *Ban dainagon e-kotoba* (Illustrated tale of Chief Councilor of State Ban), an illustrated hand scroll completed in the late twelfth century, and the *Ippen shōnin e-den* (Illustrated biography of the itinerant monk Ippen) a set of illustrated hand scrolls completed in 1299.
22. The periods mentioned are dated as follows: Nara, 710–794; Heian, 794–1185; Kamakura, 1185–1333; Keichō, 1596–1615; Genna, 1615–1624; Genroku, 1688–1704.
23. Shinsaibashi and Umeda are transit hubs and retail districts in southwest and northeast Osaka.
24. [JT] It's fine if Western women wear a *yūzen* pattern (in a Western dress) because it looks exotic, but it makes no sense for Japanese women—and especially Kansai women—to introduce Japanese tastes wholesale into their Western clothes. The well-known fashion for wearing a Mandarin coat, *happi* coat, or black silk crepe robe decorated with the family crest over a Western evening gown is something only a Westerner can carry off.
25. Presumably Tsukioka Yoshitoshi (1839–1892), master of the woodblock print.

26. Presumably Sawamura Sōjūrō VII (1875–1949).

27. [JT] I have mistakenly counted Kōshiro as a Tokyoite here. I recently learned from a newspaper article that he is a native of Ise. Kichiemon's late father, Karoku, was from the Kamigata region. And Sadanji's predecessor was from Nagoya if I'm not mistaken. I don't know the birthplace of Ennosuke's late father, Danshirō, but I do at least recall that Kikugorō IV was from Edo, as were his parents.

28. Presumably Matsumoto Kōshiro VII (1870–1949); Nakamura Kichiemon I (1886–1954); Ichikawa Ennosuke II, otherwise known as Ichikawa En'ō I (1888–1963); and Ichikawa Sadanji II (1880–1940).

29. Ichimura Uzaemon XV (1874–1945).

30. "Tsubouchi-sensei" is presumably Tsubouchi Shōyō (1859–1935), important critic. Soganoya Gorō (1877–1948), Osaka comedian.

31. Presumably Kitamura Rokurō (1871–1961).

32. Presumably Katsura Harudanji I (1878–1934), a major figure in Kamigata-style Rakugo storytelling.

33. The wide-neck shamisen is the largest of the three main types of shamisen and is commonly used by men in the Bunraku theater.

34. "Banshū" is the old domain name for the area that covers the southwestern part of present-day Hyōgo Prefecture, including Kobe.

35. "Settsu" is another old domain name, for an area that covered parts of present-day Hyōgo and Osaka Prefectures. Imazu is in the present-day city of Nishinomiya.

36. [JT] Westerners I know have told me that they find the Japanese voice lacks color, but this criticism is aimed only at the people of Kanto. The people of Kansai—that is, the people of the area from Osaka to Chūgoku—and especially the women, have wonderfully colorful voices.

37. "-asobase" is a polite feminine form of speech little used in the Kansai region.

38. *Dodoitsu* and *hauta* are genres of song often performed by geisha to shamisen accompaniment.

39. *Yasugi bushi* and *kushimoto bushi* are genres of folk song from Shimane and Wakayama prefectures, respectively.

40. [JT] The counterexample to Koutsubodayū is the late Onoe Matsunosuke (1875–1926), who, though an Osakan, became a star of the Tokyo stage. His special skill was pure Edo-style *kizewamono* (rough contemporary dramas); and even though he eliminated every trace of Osaka from his face, nevertheless there was something reminiscent of the Kamigata thickness in his voice, if you listened carefully—though perhaps this is simply my prejudice. Come to think of it, there seems to be in his acting style, too, a deeply rooted quality typical of the Kamigata region.

41. Presumably Takemoto Tsudayū III (1869–1941) and Toyotake Koutsubodayū II (1878–1967), famous chanters of the puppet theater.

42. Presumably Takemoto Settsudaijō and Takemoto Koshijidayū. Tanizaki refers to the *kamon*, an emblem or crest used to identify families, companies and, as in this case, artistic lineages, such as the Takemoto line of Bunraku chanters.

43. Takebayashi Musōan (1880–1962), novelist.

44. [JT] May Day may also be called a custom of the new age, but apart from that sort of confrontational event, it would be good also to have events at which people of all classes could forget their usual antagonism and celebrate in harmony.

45. Fujita Denzaburō (1841–1912) was founder of the Fujita zaibatsu and the first Japanese commoner to be made a baron. Tanizaki presumably refers to his son, Fujita Heitarō (1869–1940), who inherited the title.

46. [JT] Tokyo's entertainment districts have not established shopping streets free of streetcars, like Shinsaibashi-suji in Osaka, or Kyōgoku in Kyoto. In years past, there was some talk of moving the streetcar tracks that run through the Ginza district, in Tokyo, behind the shops, but it came to nothing because the shop owners were opposed, or so I heard. I cannot begin to imagine on what basis they opposed it.

47. *The River Sumida* (1911), by Nagai Kafū.

48. Tsuji Jun (1884–1944), Tokyo author, artist and anarchist.

49. [JT] In Tokyo, if one household is prosperous, it is not unusual for all their relatives to gather there and live off them. Then, the ones being taken advantage of lack the courage resolutely

to repulse their relatives, until, at last, they all end up in the poorhouse together. Such a harmful practice is rare in Osaka, since the system of main house and cadet house is strong, and they have a long practice of coming together to help each other. Both borrowers and lenders are quite cautious, and don't make such foolish agreements as people in Tokyo do. The fact that the crime of abortion is common in the Kamigata region may be attributed to the fact that families are thinking ahead to the financial consequences, whereas Tokyoites are utterly uncalculating when it comes to the birth of a child.

50. Rai San'yō (1781–1832), Confucian poet and historian, influential in the movement to restore power to the emperor.

51. Koide Narashige (1887–1931), painter and essayist.

52. [JT] When Mr. Koide died, all the major newspapers published comparatively brief obituaries. I thought sadly that there ought to have been a bit more coverage regretting the loss of such a unique local artist. It keenly brought home to me the underappreciation of the arts in Osaka.

53. Possibly for disposing of soiled toilet paper.

54. "*Uchi*" is an informal first-person pronoun; "*-hen*" is a negative ending used in Kansai dialect where standard Japanese uses "*-nai.*"

55. *Manji* (1928–30, published in Howard Hibbett's English translation as *Quicksand*).

56. Tanizaki reproduces here not only the omission of "*to*" but the polite suffix "*-haru*" and the sentence-ending "*-ten,*" both characteristic of the Kansai dialect.

57. [JT] The saying, "There are rural places in the heart of the capital" is not a paradox but the plain truth. One virtue of Kyoto is that such rural places have survived.

58. *Benshi* provided live narration for silent films.

59. Again, "Sadanji" is presumably Ichikawa Sadanji II, the famous Kabuki actor. Takada Minoru (1871–1916), was an actor of the *shinpa,* or modern, theater.

60. Presumably Prince Saionji Kinmochi (1849–1940), prime minister from 1906 to 1908 and again from 1911 to 1912. Count Kiyoura Keigo (1850–1942) was prime minister in 1924.

61. Presumably Kōda Rohan (1867–1947), author.

62. [JT] While the bourgeoisie of Tokyo depends for its livelihood upon the peerage, politicians, businessmen with political ties, senior civil servants and others associated with the worlds of politics and big business, in Osaka many merchants diligently manage their affairs through their own efforts. As a result, Tokyo government officials and important politicians tend to throw their weight around, whereas Osaka relies only on a merit system, which is nice.

63. Kaburaki Kiyokata (1878–1972), a master of Nihon-ga painting.

64. [JT] The most Tokyo-like place in Tokyo was Nihonbashi ward, but it burned to the ground in the fires after the earthquake so that not a trace remains.

65. Only thirteen years later, many of those neighborhoods would, in fact, burn down in the fire-bombings at the end of World War II, but traces remain even today around Senba.

66. Kawatake Mokuami (1816–1893), playwright of the Kabuki.

67. Two love-suicide puppet plays by Chikamatsu Monzaemon, *Meido no hikyaku* (1711) and *Shinjū ten no Amijima* (c.1720).

68. *Kanadehon Chūshingura* (1748) is the popular story of the 47 *rōnin*, or masterless samurai.

69. Kanpei, Yoichibei, O-Kaya and O-Karu are characters in *Chū-shingura*.

70. O-Sato and Sawaichi are the protagonists of *Tsubosaka reigenki* (1887). *Yoshitsune senbonzakura* (1747) sets a scene in a sushi shop in the village of Ichimura. Magoemon is a character in *Amijima*; Gonta, a character in *Yoshitsune*.

71. Sōgan is a character in *Hade sugata onna maiginu* (*A Stylish Woman's Dancing Robes*, 1772); Hachiemon, a character in *Meido no hikyaku*; and Jihei, a character in *Amijima*.

72. Wakaba no naishi is a character in *Yoshitsune*; Yaegaki-hime, a character in *Honchōnijūshikō* (*Twenty-four Examples of Filial Piety*, 1766).

73. [JT] Since the most representative fish of Japan is the sea bream, it follows that the place where sea bream is tastiest is the most Japanese part of Japan. As you travel east from Osaka, things become increasingly provincial.

In Praise of Shadows

In'ei raisan
1933

When someone with an interest in architecture has a new house built these days, it's fashionable to install the electricity, gas, water and other conveniences in such a way as to harmonize with traditional Japanese tatami-mat rooms; even those who have not built their own homes notice similar efforts when they enter a traditional room in a restaurant or inn. Although a self-sufficient master of the tea ceremony or the like, living in a thatched hut in the deepest countryside, may disregard the benefits of scientific culture, anyone living in the city with a sizable family insists upon the indoor heating, artificial light and hygienic facilities so necessary to modern life, no matter how Japanese his habits. Even the installation of a telephone torments the perfectionists, who try to find the most inconspicuous spot for it—under a staircase, say, or in the corner of the hallway. They go to such pains—having electrical lines buried in the garden, light-switches concealed in a closet or cupboard, cords secreted behind folding screens and so on—that their homes may seem fussily contrived and their efforts labored. Electric lights have already become a familiar sight, so, rather than attempting this sort of concealment, it is simpler and more natural to place an ordinary shallow opal-glass shade over the bare bulb and set it in plain view. When, as I view the passing countryside from the window of a train, I see a lonely lightbulb in such an old-fashioned shade, lit behind the sliding screen of a farmer's thatched cottage, I cannot but find it elegant. However, when it comes to electric fans, those are difficult to incorporate into a Japanese-style room, due to both their sound and their look. A person can do without them in his own home if they offend, but those in the summer hospitality business cannot simply follow their own tastes. A traditionalist friend of mine, the proprietor of the Kairakuen, detests electric fans and had long banned them from his establishment, but finally gave in after his customers complained of the summer heat. I, myself, went through similar ordeals years ago, when I spent more than I could afford on building a house and ran into various difficulties as I obsessed over every detail of the fittings and fixtures. Sliding shoji screens, for instance: as a matter of taste, I would have preferred not to insert any glass panels into them, but those covered entirely with paper are problematic for interior light and for locking up. In the end, I had the doors faced with paper on the inside and glass, unavoidably, on the outside. This necessitated sheathing on both the inside and outside of the doors, and so the expense mounted. And after all that trouble, the doors still irritate me, because, although they look like simple glass from the outside, from the inside, they lack the gentle softness of true paper shoji. I should have gone with ordinary glass doors, I think regretfully. Another person would laugh it off, but I somehow find it difficult to let such things go. Recently, electric lamps that resemble traditional paper lanterns, candlesticks and so on have come onto the market, designed to harmonize with traditional Japanese interiors, but they don't appeal to me, so I searched out old-fashioned oil lamps and paper lanterns in secondhand stores and had them electrified.

Planning for interior heating caused even more trouble. The problem is, there is not a single model of so-called gas "stove" that suits a Japanese-style interior. Furthermore, they are quite noisy, and they give me a headache unless they are equipped with a flue. In that sense, an electric heater would be ideal, but they are similarly unattractive to the eye. It would be best to obtain a heater of the sort used in street cars and conceal it in a low cupboard, but you miss that cozy, wintry feeling if you can't see the red glow of the heat, and it would be difficult for the family to gather around. After much inquiry, I had a large hearth installed, like one found in a farmhouse, and set an electric stove with artificial coals inside it. This is convenient for both boiling water and heating the room and, ignoring the expense, can be counted an aesthetic success. That was the problem of heating sorted. The next challenges were the bath and the privy. The proprietor of the Kairakuen, disdaining tiles around bathtubs and sinks, has done up his guest facilities entirely in wood. It must be admitted that tile is vastly preferable from both an economical and a practical standpoint. Still, to introduce those shiny tiles into a room where the ceiling, the beams and the wainscotting are done in fine Japanese wood absolutely ruins the overall effect. It's not so bad in my own newly built house but, as the years roll by and the beauty of the wood grain deepens, those still-glaring white tiles will look more and more out of place. Although I resolved the bath by sacrificing some convenience to aesthetics, the privy presented greater difficulties.

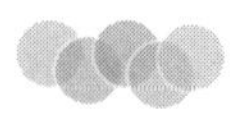

Visiting a shrine in Kyoto or Nara, I am struck with admiration for the merits of Japanese architecture whenever I am guided to the dim, old-fashioned, but nevertheless scrupulously maintained privy. A Japanese-style parlor is fine, of course, but, truly, it is in the Japanese privy that the art of repose has been perfected. No doubt that is because it is typically set some distance from the main building, in the shade of a thicket, scented by fresh leaves and moss; nothing can describe the sensation of passing down a corridor to squat in that dim light and indulge in contemplation while appreciating the faint illumination of a shoji door or gazing through a window at the garden. Mr. Sōseki counted his morning bowel movement among the pleasures of life. He called it a visceral pleasure but, beyond relishing that visceral sensation, it is a pleasure to be surrounded by restful walls and neat wooden trim and to gaze at blue sky and verdure—surely there can be no place more suitable for it than a Japanese-style privy. To these I would add the following indispensable features: the combination of a certain gloom and scrupulous sanitation, as I have said already, and a silence pierced only by the buzz of an occasional mosquito. I like to relax in such a privy and listen to the gently falling rain. I especially like privies in the Kanto region, with slots at the floor for sweeping out dust; through the slots one can hear, that much closer, the gentle sound of the raindrops falling from the eaves and the tree leaves to bathe the foot of a stone lantern and moisten the mossy rocks before soaking into the earth. Indeed, a privy is the most appropriate place to hear the sounds of insects and songs of birds, and, on a moonlit night, to savor the ephemeral charms of each season in turn; surely the ancient poets came up with many of their subjects there.

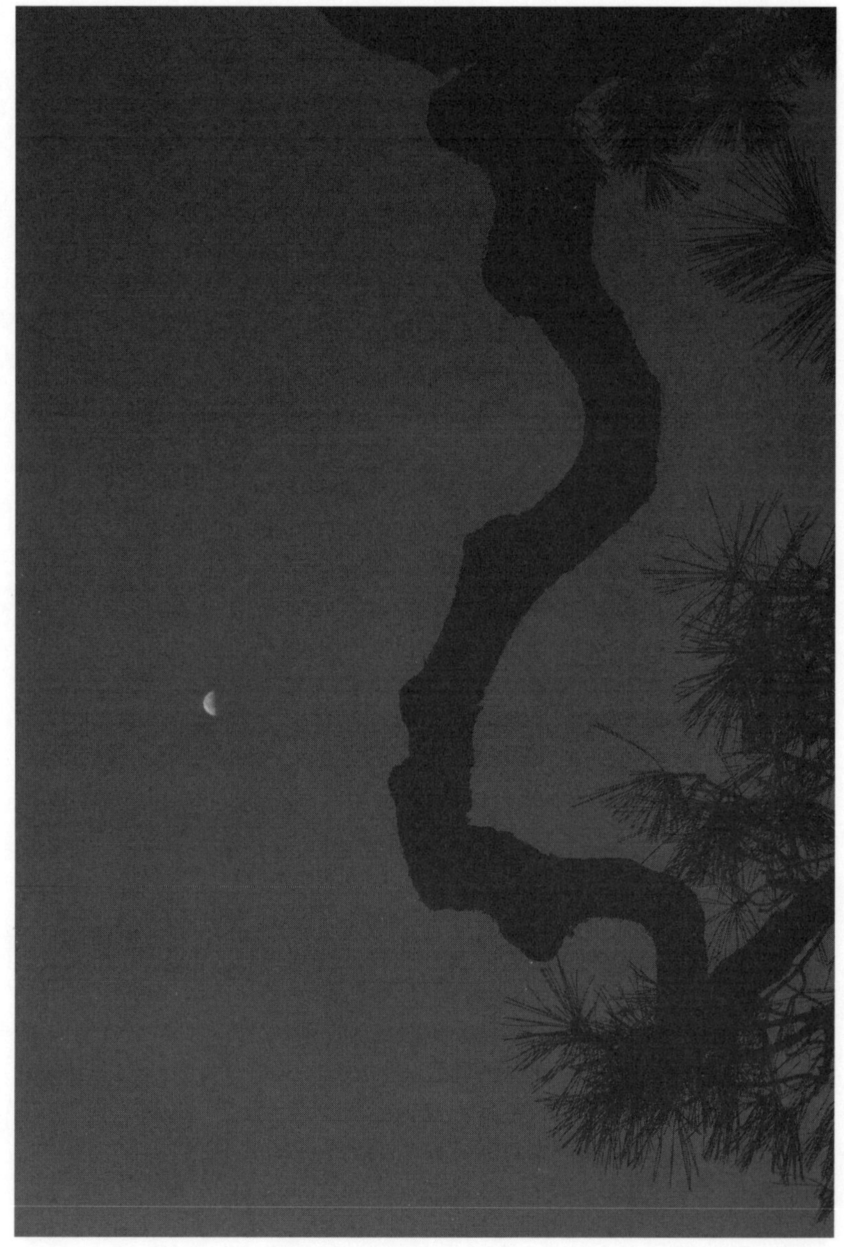

Therefore, it is no overstatement to say that the privy is the most elegant product of Japanese architecture. Our ancestors, who made of everything poetry, took what ought to be the filthiest place in the house and transformed it into a place of artistry instead, where they communed with the beauties of nature and enveloped themselves in nostalgic associations. Compared to Westerners, who thinks of the toilet as something unclean and avoid even speaking of it in company, we are far more reasonable on this matter and truly grasp the essence of refinement. If forced to admit some deficiency of the Japanese privy, I would say that setting it apart from the main part of the house makes a nighttime visit inconvenient and, especially in the winter, raises the fear of catching cold, but, just as Saitō Ryokuu has stated, "Elegance is a thing of the cold," and that sort of place should be as chilly as the outdoors. The steam heat of a Western-style hotel lavatory is truly disturbing. Everyone with a taste for sukiya-style traditional architecture idealizes the Japanese privy, but few people have a house as big as a temple, or so many hands to do the housekeeping, and in an ordinary house it is no simple matter to keep such a privy always spotless. In particular, if the floor is done with wooden boards or tatami mats, the dirt will eventually show, no matter how careful you are or how diligently you clean. If you tile the floor instead, and install a flush toilet and modern plumbing, it is not only more hygienic but easier to keep clean; on the other hand, you completely sever any connection with "elegance" or "the beauties of nature." In such a space—glaringly illuminated and, what's worse, surrounded by four whiter-than-white walls—it's difficult to enjoy fully what Mr. Sōseki called a visceral pleasure. Certainly, it is sanitary to have every corner of the room pure white, but there is no need to call such attention to the spot where we eliminate waste from our body. Just as it is improper for a woman to expose her buttocks or her feet, no matter how beautiful her skin, to illuminate the toilet so revealingly is vulgar in the extreme; while what you can see may look sanitary, it also provokes associations with what you cannot see. After all, it is better if such a place is shrouded in murky beams of dim light that blur the distinction between the clean and the dirty. For this reason, when I had my own house built, although I opted for modern plumbing, I absolutely refused to have white tiling and tried to give the privy a Japanese atmosphere with a floor of camphor-wood planks. The toilet bowl presented the only difficulty. As the reader knows, toilet bowls come only in pure-white porcelain, equipped with glittering chrome hardware. What I required, ideally, was both a men's toilet and a women's toilet made of wood. Black-lacquered wood would be the ultimate luxury, but even plain wood would darken to an appropriate blackness as the months and years passed, lending to the grain an oddly soothing loveliness. In particular, it must be admitted that a wooden urinal laid with branches of cryptomeria is perfect, not only for its refreshing appearance but for the way it muffles the slightest sound. While I could not aspire to such luxury, I thought I might at least have my preferred sort of toilet made and installed, but to custom-order something like that would have taken a great deal of time and money, and I had to give it up. So, the process of building my house involved various compromises, whether in regard to the lighting, or the heating, or the plumbing; and while I did not object to adopting the conveniences of civilization, even so, part of me wondered whether we

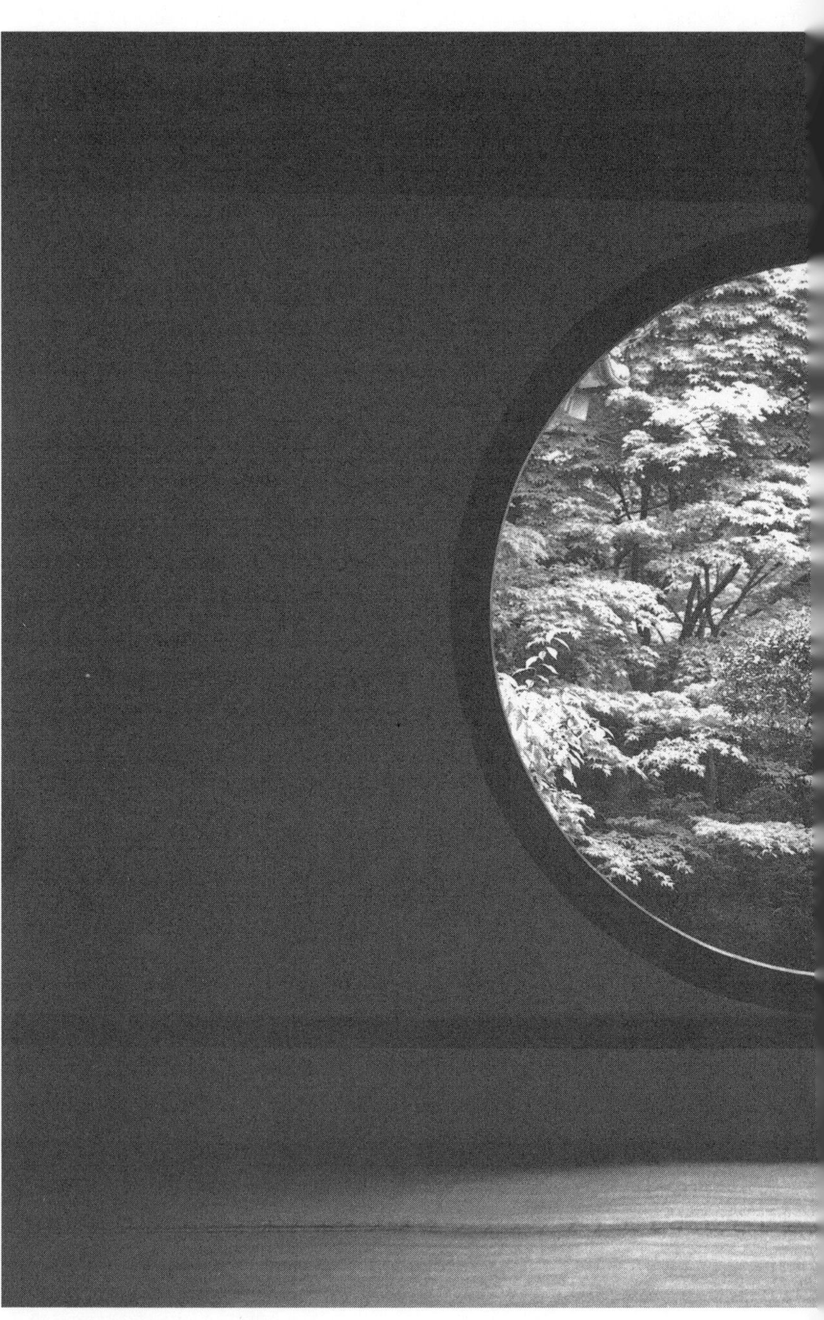

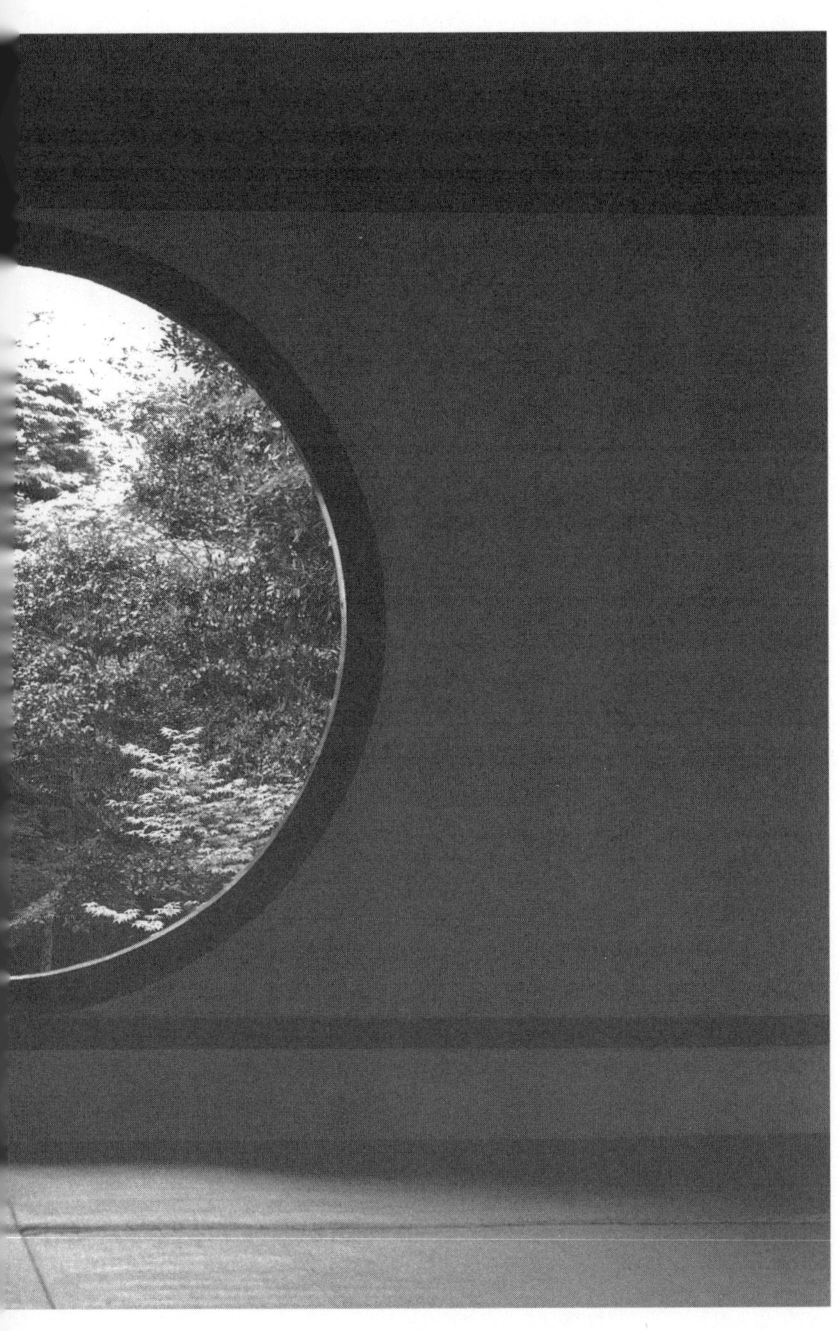

might better honor our own customs and practices by adapting those conveniences to accord with them.

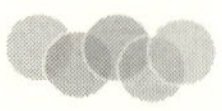

The recent fad for electric lamps in the style of a traditional *andon* with a paper shade results from our having reawakened to the once-forgotten gentleness and warmth of paper, and it demonstrates our recognition that paper suits the Japanese house better than glass; and yet toilets and heaters of a similarly appropriate style still have not appeared on the market. As for heating, the solution I came up with seems best: an electric "coal" heater set within a hearth. Still, no one will take the trouble to produce such a simple product (one does find flimsy electric heaters, but those are, like an ordinary hibachi, inadequate for indoor heating). Unsightly Western-style stoves are the only things readily available. Of course, it is a luxury to worry so about taste in such trivialities of everyday life. Some say that, so long as we can avoid extremities of heat and cold and starvation, we have no right to pursue style. It is difficult to deny ourselves the comforts of life; no matter how we try, "snowy nights still feel cold" (as the Buddhist proverb acknowledges), and when we see some useful tool right before our eyes, we surrender to the overwhelming desire to enjoy its benefits, without wasting time debating its elegance or inelegance. Be that as it may, I often wonder how different the conditions of our society would be if a unique scientific culture had developed in the East, completely distinct from that of the West. If, for example, we possessed our own physics, our own chemistry, would we not, in due time, have achieved advancements in engineering and industry based upon them, and would those advancements not have produced all sorts of products—appliances of every kind for use in daily life, and medicines, and handicrafts—that better conform to our national character? Not only that; more than likely, we would have come to an understanding, different from the West's, of the very principles of physics, of chemistry, an understanding that would reveal the nature and the potential of light rays, electricity and the atom in different terms from those in which we now think. I don't understand such scientific principles; I am just indulging in aimless fantasies. Still, if innovations in at least the practical fields had taken a more independent path, that could not help but exert a powerful influence, not only on style in the necessities of daily life, of course, but on our politics, religion, arts, industry and more, so one readily infers that the East, as the East, might have unlocked an alternate universe. As a mundane example: I once published a comparison of the fountain pen and the calligraphy brush in the journal *Bungei shunjū*, in which I suggested that, if a Japanese or Chinese person of old had invented the fountain pen, it would have had a brush at the tip rather than a nib. And then the ink would not have been blue but something closer to the color of India ink, devised to flow from the shaft into the bristles of the brush. In that case, Western paper wouldn't do, so something close to *washi* paper or other calligraphy paper would have been put into mass production to answer the extreme demand. If Japanese paper and India ink and writing brushes had developed in this way, then fountain pens and Western ink would not be as fashionable as they are today; consequently, the movement for adopting the alphabet would not wield such influence, and affection for kanji and the kana writing systems would be far stronger. More than that, our thought and our literature, instead of so thoroughly imitating that of the West, might push forward into new and original territories. If you think about it, though it is merely stationery, its influence is infinitely great.

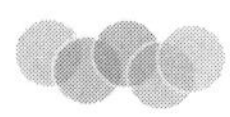

Such thoughts are a novelist's fancies; now that this day has dawned, we cannot go back and start over. I fully recognize that. Therefore, at this stage, my words are no more than wishing for the impossible and complaining about how things are. But as I'm grumbling, I might as well consider just how much we have lost, compared to Westerners. To put it simply, the West has followed a reasonable path to arrive at the present while we, confronted with a superior culture, have had to follow them, abandoning our own path, which had developed over the past several millennia. This has seemingly led to various accidents and inconveniences. Left to our own devices, we might have experienced no significant progress over the last five hundred years. In truth, if you visit the countryside of China or India, people there probably lead lives little different from the time of Confucius or the Buddha, but that is simply because they have followed the only way suited to their nature. Although their progress may be slow, as it continues step by step, they may one day invent modern "conveniences" that are genuinely convenient for themselves, in place of those things borrowed from another culture, such as today's train, airplane, or radio. Consider the cinema, and how the tonalities and the use of shadow in an American movie differ so from a French or German movie. Apart from the acting and the plotting, the national character somehow emerges from the camera lens itself. This is the case even though each nation's filmmakers use exactly the same equipment, chemicals and film. Think, then, if we had our own native photographic arts, suited to our skin, our features, our land's climate and topography! Or consider the gramophone and the radio: if we had invented them, how well might they highlight the best aspects of our voices and our music. Because our music is an art of understatement and mood, it loses most of its charm when recorded and amplified. When it comes to the art of conversation, too, we keep our voices low, our words few. Above all, we value the intervals between words; but intervals completely perish when speaking over the telephone. Therefore, we bend our arts to accommodate the machine. Westerners on the other hand need not do so because those machines were developed by them and naturally suit their arts. I believe that, in this sense, we have suffered manifold losses.

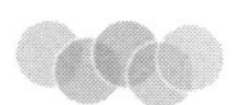

I've heard that paper is a Chinese invention. While Western-style paper inspires in us no more of an emotional response than any other simple everyday item, Chinese or Japanese paper causes us to feel a certain warmth when we see its texture, and this soothes our heart. Even if both are white, the whiteness of Chinese or Japanese paper is different from that of Western paper. The surface of Western paper reflects light, while Chinese or Japanese paper is fleecy and absorbs the light like winter's first gentle snowfall. It has a supple texture, and it makes no sound when torn or

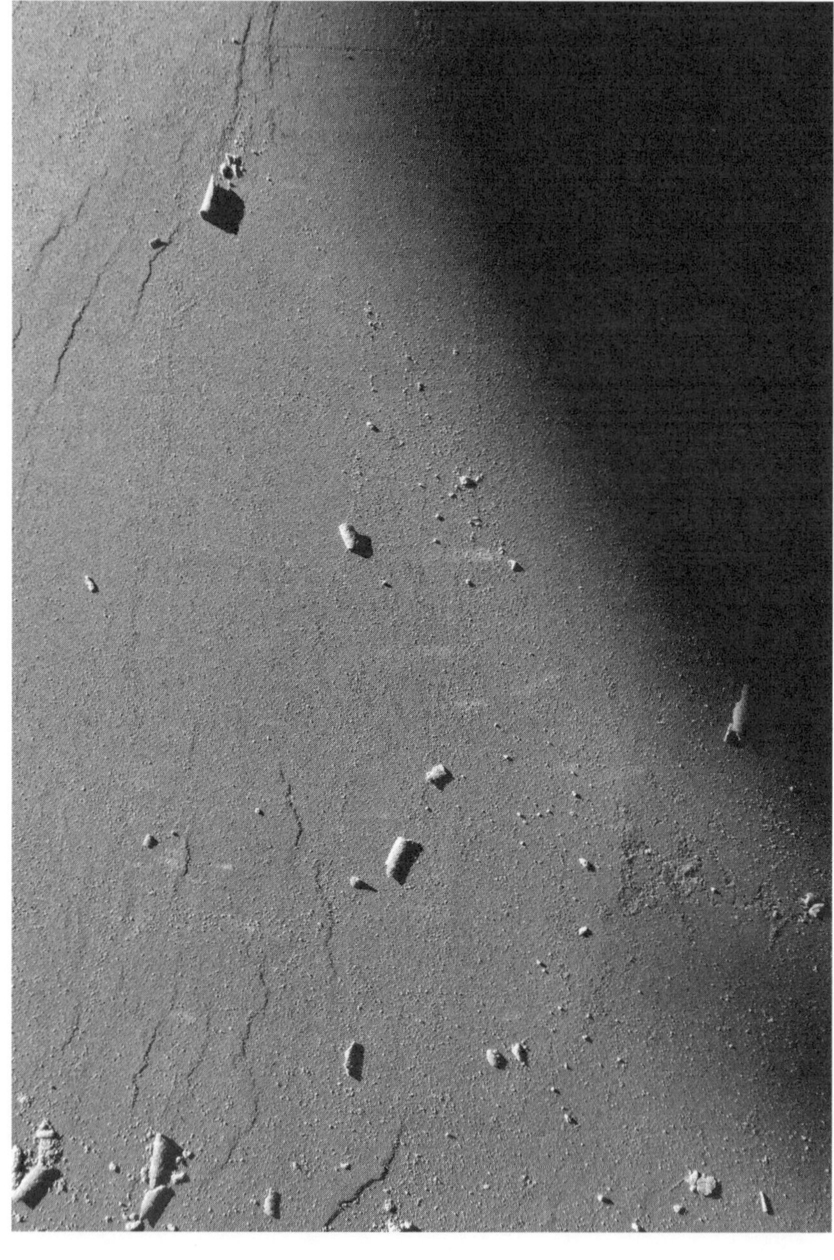

folded. Its touch is as gentle and mellow as tree leaves. In the first place, we Easterners cannot relax around things that sparkle. At table, Westerns use utensils made of silver, steel, or nickel, polished to a shine, but we dislike that sort of glitter. We do sometimes use kettles, sake cups, or decanters made of silver, but we do not polish them. On the contrary, we are glad when the initial shine dulls, the tarnish deepens and the age begins to show; in any house here, an ignorant maid has been scolded by her master for mistakenly polishing away the carefully cultivated patina of some silver tableware. Recently, among Chinese people, dishware made of tin has come into general use; I suppose they appreciate that it takes on an antiqued look. When new, it isn't very nice, rather resembling aluminum, and the Chinese won't accept it until it has acquired some age and elegance. Moreover, those dishes are engraved with lines of poetry, so they come to look quite appropriate as the surface darkens. In the hands of the Chinese, even a cheap, shiny metal such as tin gains the profundity, sobriety and dignity of pottery. Chinese also love jade, and surely it is only we Asians who feel a fascination for that lumpy stone, possessed of such a mysteriously cloudy glow that radiates, dull and slow, from its deepest interior, as though the ancient atmosphere of centuries were condensed within it. We, ourselves, hardly understand where we acquired a love for such a stone, which possesses neither the deep color of a ruby or emerald nor the brilliance of a diamond. But looking at its hazy surface, it seems a truly Chinese stone; it seems that the sediment of Chinese culture with its long history is accumulated within that profound opacity, and it hardly seems strange that the Chinese should prefer such a substance, such a color and luster. Recently, a great deal of rock crystal is imported from Chile, but compared with Japanese crystal, it is too pure and clear. We have long valued crystals that, though clear, retain a faint cloudiness throughout that lends gravity, and the Japanese crystals that contain fragments of grass or other occlusions delight us. Even glass—is not the glass developed in the Qianlong era (1735–1796) closer to jade or agate in appearance? There must be some important connection with our national character in the fact that, although the method of manufacturing glass was understood early in the East, it died out without developing as it did in the West, while ceramics flourished. It is not that we hate all bright things as a rule, but we prefer deep shadow to superficial brilliance. Whether it is natural stones or manmade wares, we always choose those with an opacity that calls to mind the mellow luster of age. One often hears this expression, "the luster of age," and what it really means is the shine that comes from constant handling. Both Chinese and Japanese have words for the luster that develops as people stroke one spot on an object over long months and years and the oil from their hands naturally suffuses it. As I come to think about it, just as it is said that "elegance is a thing of the cold," it is also "a thing of grime." At any rate, we cannot deny that the concept of "elegance" in which we delight includes a somewhat grimy and unhygienic element. If the Westerner uproots and exposes dirt and removes it, the Easterner carefully preserves and glorifies it. Well, it may be a kind of loser's rationalization but, out of necessity, we love things stained by the dirt of humanity, by the soot of the lamp, by the wind and rain, and the shade and luster that calls all that to mind, and we can relax and sooth our nerves living in that sort of building, surrounded by those sorts of wares. In that regard, I often think that hospital walls, surgical uniforms and medical equipment, if they are intended for Japanese patients, should be not all white and bright, but a bit darker and softer in tone. If the walls of the room were sand-coated and the floors covered in tatami mats, the patient receiving treatment would certainly be calmer. One reason we hate to visit the dentist is the grinding sound, of course, but another is the excess of shiny glass and metal—that's what frightens us. When I was suffering from neurasthenia, someone recommended a dentist recently returned from America, whose office boasted the latest equipment—a hair-raising prospect! Instead, I decided to visit a rather behind-the-times dentist who had set up his office in an old-fashioned Japanese house of the sort found in provincial towns. Of course, antiquated medical equipment presents a problem, too. I suppose if modern medical techniques had developed in Japan, the instruments and equipment for treating patients would have been contrived to better suit Japanese-style rooms. This is one more example of the losses we have suffered by borrowing.

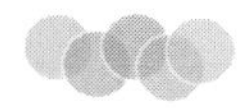

There is a well-known restaurant in Kyoto called the Waranjiya that refused to install electric lights in their dining rooms, using candles instead, and this was part of their appeal, but when I visited last spring after a long absence, they had begun to use electric lamps designed to look like traditional *andon* lanterns. I asked when they had made the change and was told, "Last year. Many customers complained that candlelight was too weak, so management had no choice." However, the staff will still bring a candle for those customers who prefer it. I had come there precisely to enjoy candlelight, so I asked them to switch out my electric lamp and, when they did, I noticed how the dim, indistinct light revealed the beauty of the Japanese lacquerware. The Waranjiya serves diners in snug little tea-ceremony rooms of just four and a half mats, each with an alcove and ceiling of lustrous blackened wood. The room is dark even when illuminated by electrified lantern, but by replacing that with a candle, immersing the serving trays and lacquer bowls in its flaring, flickering light, I discovered a completely different fascination emanating from their sheen, deep and profound as a lacquer swamp. Thus we see it was not by mere coincidence that our ancestors discovered the material called lacquer and came to love the look of lacquerware. My friend Mr. Sabarwal tells me that in India, even today, people scorn the use of stoneware for dishes and instead use mostly lacquerware. We, on the other hand, use lacquerware for serving trays and soup bowls, but otherwise use mostly stoneware, unless is it for the tea ceremony or another such ritual purpose. Lacquerware has a reputation as rather unsophisticated and inelegant, and I think one reason may be the brightness of today's interiors, flooded as they are with both natural and artificial light. Honestly, darkness is an essential condition for appreciating its beauty. Although something called "white lacquer" has recently appeared, lacquer has traditionally been black, brown, or red, and the darkness of these colors, built up layer upon layer, is something born inevitably from the surrounding shade. Small decorative boxes or inkstands or display shelves of highly polished *maki-e* lacquer, with eye-catching gold or silver inlay, are indeed garish and unsettling, and may seem merely vulgar, but cast them into deepest shade, replace the brightness of the sun or of electric lights with a single votive or candle, and in an instant that garish object sinks into the shade, growing quiet and dignified. The craftspeople of ancient times must have imagined just such a dark room when they painted these objects with lacquer and decorated them with gold; they aimed at the effect the objects would have in such meager light, gauging the manner in which the gold they applied so lavishly would emerge from the shade and the degree to which it would reflect the candlelight. In other words, *maki-e* lacquerware should not be seen in a bright room, where the gold inlay is revealed all at once, but in a dark space, where the various details catch the light little by little, here and there, while most of the gorgeous decoration remains concealed by shadow; then, it makes an indescribable impression. Likewise, the shiny lacquer surface: placed in a dark space, perhaps reflecting the flickering flame of a candle, the reflection lagging just behind the occasional movement of air that stirs even in a still room, it invites one to meditate upon it without knowing why. If the dim room were empty of lacquerware, how diminished would be the glamour of that dreamworld of uncertain light engendered by the candle, that evening pulse that the flicker of light beats. The lacquerware captures each flicker, now here now there, lightly, faintly, minutely weaving the pattern etched in silver onto the night itself, just as if the surface of the tatami mats were crossed and dotted with streams and small ponds. Certainly, stoneware makes for fine dishes, too, but it has no shading, no depth. Stoneware is heavy and cold to the touch. Moreover, it conducts heat quickly, so it is unsuitable for serving hot food, and it makes a clattering noise when you set it down, whereas lacquerware is light and warm to the touch, and does not offend the ear. There is nothing I love better than the cozy warmth I feel as I pick up a lacquer soup bowl and my palm senses the weight of the broth. It feels something like cradling the wobbly little body of a newborn baby. This is one powerful reason why soup bowls are still made from lacquer; a ceramic bowl cannot convey the same sense. If clear soup is served in a ceramic bowl, you see all the contents and the play of colors the moment you remove the lid. But if the bowl is lacquerware, there is a moment, after you remove the lid and as you lift the bowl to your mouth, when you stare into the liquid, hardly different in color from the bowl itself, as it soundlessly settles into its dark, profound depths. You cannot see whether anything lies in the darkness of the bowl's interior, but your hands sense the sway of the broth in the bowl, the slight condensation on its rim, and then you recognize the steam rising from it, and this steam, via the scent it carries, delicately presages the flavor before you take the first sip. What a difference, when we compare the mood of that moment to the Western practice of serving soup in a shallow, white dish. It might be called a kind of mystery—even a moment of zen.

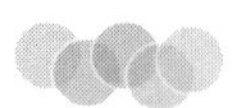

A lacquer soup bowl sitting before me rings with a sound, "*jii*," that seems faintly to penetrate the inner ear. Listening to that sound, like the distant call of an insect, quiets my anticipation of whatever I am about to eat, reliably drawing me into a state of no-self. Masters of tea ceremony are said to enter a state of self-renunciation as the sound of the boiling water calls up associations with the wind in the

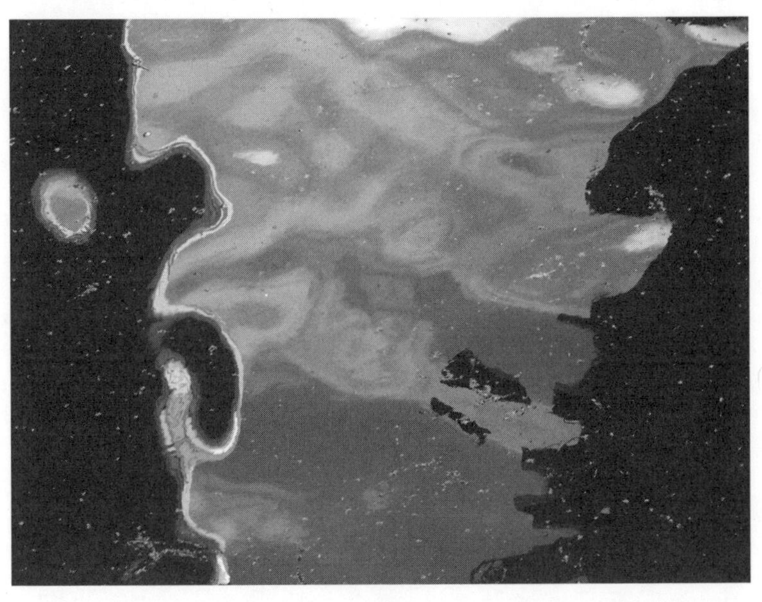

famous Onoe pine tree at Takasago; I imagine it is rather like that. Japanese food is said to be something to see rather than to eat, and in this case, I think it something to contemplate—the silent music produced, in ensemble, by the lacquer vessel and the scintillating flame of the candle in the dark. Mr. Sōseki praised the color of *yōkan* red-bean jelly in his novel *Kusamakura* (*The Three-Cornered World,* 1906), and, indeed, that color has a meditative quality. The cloudy, semi-transparent surface, like jade, seems to absorb the sun's rays into its interior, so that biting into it feels dreamlike, as if one is biting into the dimmed light. Such depth and complexity of color is absolutely unknown in Western sweets. How naïve and one-dimensional whipped cream seems, by comparison! Place that *yōkan* into the darkness of a lacquerware box, the color of which is hardly distinguishable from that of the sweet, and it becomes still more meditative. Taking the cool, smooth piece of *yōkan* into the mouth, the darkness of the room becomes a sweet lump melting on the tongue, and the *yōkan*, which is not really that tasty, gains a strange depth of flavor. Certainly, the colors of any country's cuisine are contrived to harmonize with its customary tableware and interiors, and so to serve Japanese cuisine on stark white dishes in a brightly lit room renders it only half as appetizing. For example, if we consider the color of the red-miso soup we eat each morning, we recognize it as a product of the dimly lit Japanese houses of old. Once, when I was invited to a tea ceremony and served miso soup, in the unsteady light of a candle, settling to the bottom of a black lacquer bowl, the red-clay color of that familiar broth became truly profound and appealing. Or consider soy sauce. People in the Kamigata region use a dark soy sauce called tamari on sashimi, pickled vegetables and boiled greens. How rich in shadow, how appropriate to the darkness that viscous, lustrous sauce is! At the same time, various pale-colored foods—white miso, tofu, *kamaboko* fish paste, grated-yam soup, or white-fish sashimi—gain nothing from being served in brightly-lit surroundings. White rice, for one thing, looks more beautiful and more appetizing when placed in a gleaming black-lacquer serving dish and set in a dark space. Surely every Japanese person appreciates its value when they remove the lid of a black lacquer bowl and see the freshly cooked, pure white rice inside, warm steam rising from it, each grain gleaming like a pearl. If we think of it in this way, we realize that our cuisine always sustains a base note of shadow and an inseparable relation to darkness.

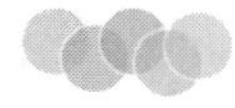

I am a complete layman when it comes to architecture, but I understand that the beauty of the gothic architecture of Western churches is said to lie in the vaulted roof that rises high into the sky. The Buddhist temples of our country, on the other hand, are covered by a low, tiled roof, the eaves of which cast the entire structure into a broad, deep shade. Not only temples, but palaces and commoners' houses too: the most distinctive elements of our buildings, as seen from outside, are the wide tiled or thatched roof and the dense darkness that spreads beneath it. Sometimes, even in midday, the entryway, door, walls, or pillars are hardly discernable in the cave-like shade beneath the eaves. It is true of most buildings of former times, both magnificent temples such as Chion-in or Honganji and farmhouses in the bosky countryside, that the roof seems greater in

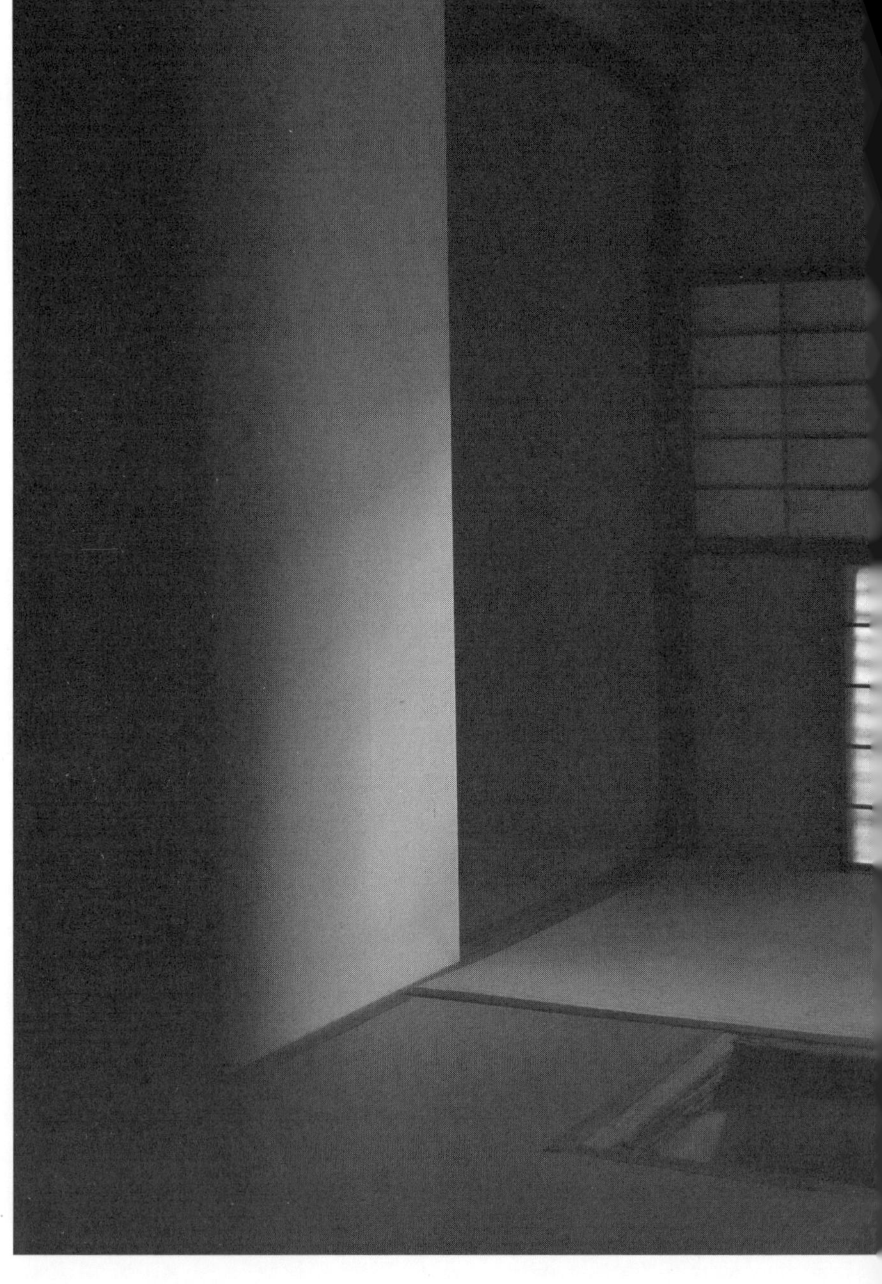

weight, height and overall area, at least to the eye, than everything underneath. We Japanese first open a sort of parasol called a roof, casting an area of the ground into shade, and then build our house in the dimness of that shadow. Western houses have roofs too, of course, but their primary purpose is to provide shelter from bad weather rather than from the sun. They are designed to produce as little shade as possible, and from the outside you can tell that the interior receives as much light as possible. If the Japanese roof is a parasol, the Western roof is nothing more than a cap—specifically a newsboy cap, with the smallest possible visor, to allow the sun's rays to reach deep beneath. Various factors, including climate and weather, building materials and so on certainly influenced the width of the eaves on the traditional Japanese house. For example, since brick, glass and cement are not used in the construction, such wide eaves are necessary to protect the sides of the house from wind and rain. Even Japanese people would find a bright room more convenient than a dark one, of course, but it has unavoidably turned out otherwise. However, since beauty always develops from the realities of everyday life, our ancestors, who lived of necessity in dark rooms, unwittingly discovered beauty in shadow and, before long, came to use shadow to attain the goal of beauty. In truth, the beauty of a traditional Japanese tatami room is born solely from the nuance of shadow. It is natural for Westerners to be surprised by the simplicity of such a room and to feel it is nothing more than four gray walls devoid of ornamentation, but that is because they do not understand the enigma of shadow. As if that were not enough, around the outside of the traditional room, which the rays of the sun pierce only with difficulty, we extend verandas and exterior breezeways, pushing the sunlight even farther away. And then, the reflected light from the garden barely filters through the paper shoji screens and creeps into the room. We intentionally paint our rooms in weak colors, as though these feeble, dreary, fleeting sunbeams had quietly settled down and soaked into the walls. We apply a glossy finish to the walls of the storehouse, the kitchen, or the hallway, but the walls of the tatami room are almost always coated in a sandy finish and not allowed to shine. If they were, then the soft, frail flavor of those meager sunbeams would be extinguished. Come what may, people like us enjoy the delicate glow of apparently weak natural light that clings to the surface of the dusky-colored wall, eking out its last moments of life. For us, this light on the walls, now bright, now dim, surpasses any ornamentation, and we never tire of it. Naturally, then, we paint those sandy walls in a solid color, without pattern, to avoid competing with the light, and though the colors vary from room to room, how subtle the difference! Rather than a difference in color, it is really nothing more than the slightest variation in tone and in the mood of the observer. Moreover, according to that variation, the shadows in each room take on a slightly different tone. It is true that our tatami rooms include a tokonoma alcove, where we set flower arrangements and hang scrolls featuring paintings or calligraphy, but those serve not to ornament so much as to lend depth to the shadow. When hanging a scroll, we strive, above all else, to strike a harmony with the tokonoma wall—what we call *toko-utsuri.* We place as much importance on the mounting of a scroll as on the calligraphy or picture itself, so that, really, if the mounting does not suit the tokonoma, then the hanging is a failure, no matter how great a work of calligraphy it

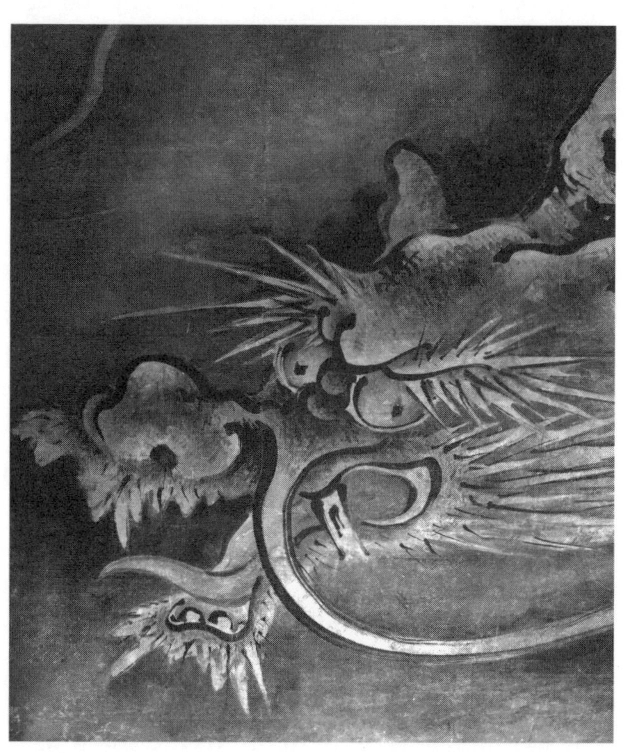

frames. On the other hand, one might take a painting or sample of calligraphy that, on its own, is no great work of art and try placing it in the tokonoma to find that it works quite well there, such that both the scroll and the room suddenly come to life. And if we ask what it is about such a scroll, unremarkable in itself, that harmonizes so well, it is invariably the faded colors of the backing paper, ink and fabric used in the mounting. Those colors strike just the right balance with the darkness of the alcove or the room. We often visit famous temples in Kyoto or Nara where we are shown a treasured scroll displayed in the deep inner alcove of a great hall. Because the alcove is dark even at midday, we can hardly make out anything, and so we simply listen to the docent, peer at the faint traces of the ink, and imagine what a masterpiece it must be. Nevertheless, the obscurity of the ancient scroll accords perfectly with the darkness of the tokonoma. Indeed, the indistinctness of the image, far from a problem, seems appropriate. For in this case, the picture is nothing more than a distinguished surface for catching the weak and faltering light, serving just the same function as the sand-coated walls. Here lies the reason that we prize age and "patina" when choosing a hanging scroll: a new picture, even one done with ink wash or pale colors, may destroy the shadow of the tokonoma, unless chosen with care.

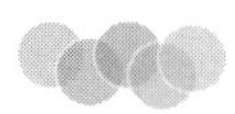

If we think of a tatami room as an ink-wash painting, then shoji screens are the area of the painting where the ink wash is faintest, and the tokonoma, the area where it is darkest. Whenever I see the tokonoma in a Japanese-style tatami room of concentrated refinement, I marvel that Japanese people possess such a thorough understanding of the mysteries of shadow and such skill in differentiating light and shade. It requires no special furnishings; just neat and tidy walls and woodwork enclosing and isolating a space, the dim corners animated here and there by sunbeams lured into its emptiness. Nevertheless, we gaze at the darkness behind the lintel, around the vase, or beneath the display shelf and, while recognizing that it is merely shadow, we are deeply moved by a sense that the atmosphere is quietly settling just there, and an eternal and unchanging peace is possessing the darkness. I presume that Westerners, when they speak of "the inscrutable East," are referring to this uncanny silence of the darkness. Even we Japanese remember as children being chilled by an indescribable terror when we stared into the depths of the tokonoma or the Japanese-style study, into which sunlight never penetrated. And what is the key to this inscrutability? The secret, after all, lies in the magic of shadow. If we expelled the shadows from every corner, the tokonoma would suddenly become nothing more than a void. The genius of our ancestors was to preserve a quality of *yūgen,* surpassing any mural or other ornamentation, in the shadow world produced naturally by the arbitrary isolation of a space of nothingness. Though this seems a simple technique, in fact it is not so easy to accomplish. For example, it is difficult to imagine the unseen effort that goes into determining each detail of the tokonoma's design—the shape of the window in the study nook, the thickness of the lintel, the height of the threshold—yet I stop in front of it, amid the dim, pale light from the study nook, and I forget the passage of time. Such windows were originally designed to facilitate reading, as the name "study" suggests, but at some point came to serve to illuminate the tokonoma, or, rather than illuminate it, mostly to filter the slanting light from the nook through the paper shoji, suitably dampening it. Indeed, what a chilly, miserable light glows from the backlit paper! The sunlight from the garden, having slipped under the eaves and traversed the veranda, finally reaches the shoji, its power to light an object exhausted, its heat dissipated, and can only wanly highlight the color of the paper screen. Again and again, I stop before such shoji and stare at the paper surface, bright but not in the least dazzling. In the great hall of a Buddhist temple, since the garden is so far away, the sunbeams are that much more diluted, so that winter, spring, summer, or fall; in cloudy weather or fine; at morning, noon, or evening; there is no variation in the dimness. And the paper is permanently stained as though dirt had accumulated in each and every corner of the grid-like shoji frame, so that one suspects they may no longer open and close. At such moments, I blink in wonder at the dreamlike light. Something shimmers hazily before my eyes, and I feel my vision grow dull. That is because the dimly white reflections from the paper screen, just lacking the power to drive away the rich darkness of the tokonoma and instead being repelled by it, reveal a world of bewilderment where light and dark are indistinguishable. Have you, dear reader, never walked into a Japanese style room and sensed that the sunbeams floating through it were different from ordinary sunbeams—that they were solemn things, benisons? Have you never felt a kind of horror of eternity, as though you lost all sense of the passage of time while in that room, months and years elapsing without your notice, to find when you emerged that you had grown old and gray?

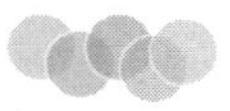

Then, dear reader, have you never gone to a room deep in the interior of some great edifice and found there, amid a darkness seemingly untouched by the light outside, a gold-decorated panel or screen that has caught the tip of a sunbeam from the distant garden and reflects it like a quickening dream? The reflection casts a weak golden glow onto the surrounding darkness, like the twilit horizon, and never has gold looked so mournful. You turn to reexamine it several times as you pass by and, as your perspective shifts from head-on to sideways, the gold paper on the surface slowly glows from within—not with a twinkle or a busy sparkle, but rather with a protracted gleam, like a giant's blush. Perhaps you walk around the side of the screen and discover that some flakes of gold that had, until now, reflected the light only lazily, as if half-asleep, are glittering like a flame, and you marvel that the gold has gathered so many sunbeams in such a dark place. That is when I understand for the first time why the people of the past used gold to decorate statues of the Buddha and the walls of aristocrats' rooms. People today, living in brightly lit houses, cannot comprehend this sort of golden beauty. The people of old, living in dark houses, were not simply enchanted by the color, though; I believe they understood its practical value, too. After all, gold serves as a reflector of sunlight in such light-starved interiors. In short, gold foil and gold dust served them not simply as a luxury but as a means to reflect and thereby supplement the available light. If that is the case, then we can grasp the reason that gold, which brightens dark rooms with its persistent glow, has been peculiarly valued above silver and other metals that soon lose their luster. Above I wrote that *maki-e* lacquerware was made to be seen in a dark room; we can extend this line of thinking to other old-fashioned crafts, such as fabrics lavishly woven with gold and silver threads. Is there a better example than the gold-brocade stoles worn by monks? These days, most of the temples all across town generally keep their main hall well-lit for the public; in such spaces the gold brocade seems pointlessly gaudy, and its merit is absolutely incomprehensible—no matter how dignified the priest wearing it. If, however, you attend rites at a venerable temple that keeps to the old ways, then you will understand how that gold-brocade cape perfectly harmonizes with the wrinkled face and hands of the aged priest and the flickering light of the votive candles before the Buddha, and how much it contributes to the overall magnificence, and that is because, just as with *maki-e* lacquerware, most of the gaudy pattern is obscured by the darkness, with only small fragments of the gold and silver threads glittering here and there. Furthermore, nothing so well suits the Japanese complexion as the costumes of the Noh theater (though it may be only myself who thinks so). Needless to say, many of those costumes are quite ornate, abundantly decorated with gold and silver, and Noh actors, unlike their counterparts in the Kabuki theater, do not paint their faces white, so the costumes flatter the reddish brown skin characteristic of most Japanese and the ivory color of some faces, tinged with amber in a way one sees nowhere else; I admire it every time I go to watch Noh. Heian-style costumes woven or embroidered with gold and silver suit the Japanese complexion, but so do the simpler sorts of costumes in deep green or persimmon, plain white under-kimono and the like. Sometimes, when a beautiful youth wears such a costume, it sets off still more the complexion of his cheeks, with their smoothness and youthful glow; then one can see with full comprehension the allure, naturally different from that of a woman's skin, and understand, "Ah! This is how the daimyo of old were conquered by the beauty of their favorite boy." In the Kabuki theater, too, the magnificence of the costumes for the period dramas or dance-plays is by no means inferior, but, although the Kabuki is considered to exceed Noh in sex appeal, if you attend both frequently, you come to realize that in fact the opposite is true. I don't dispute that, if you have but little experience of each, then Kabuki seems to possess more eroticism and more prettiness—or that it did in the old days, at any rate. But those gaudy colors tend to slip into vulgarity when viewed on contemporary stages lit Western-style, and they become exhausting. If it's true of the costumes, it's equally true of the makeup; the completely made-up face of Kabuki, even granting its beauty, conveys no real sense of *natural* beauty. Whereas the Noh actor takes the stage with his face, neck and hands free of makeup, so his magnetism lies entirely in the person himself and not in any sort of visual deception. Therefore, in Noh, one never loses interest in the actor playing the role of a lover or a woman just because one gets too close. Rather, we feel only wonder at how splendid he looks when dressed in those gaudy period costumes that, at first glance, would seem not to suit someone like him, with the same skin color as us. I once saw Mr. Kongō Iwao assay the role of Yang Guifei in the Noh play *Kōtei* (The emperor), and I still cannot forget the beauty of his arm peeking from its sleeve.[1] Watching his hand, I thought constantly about my own hand resting on my lap. His hand looked so beautiful

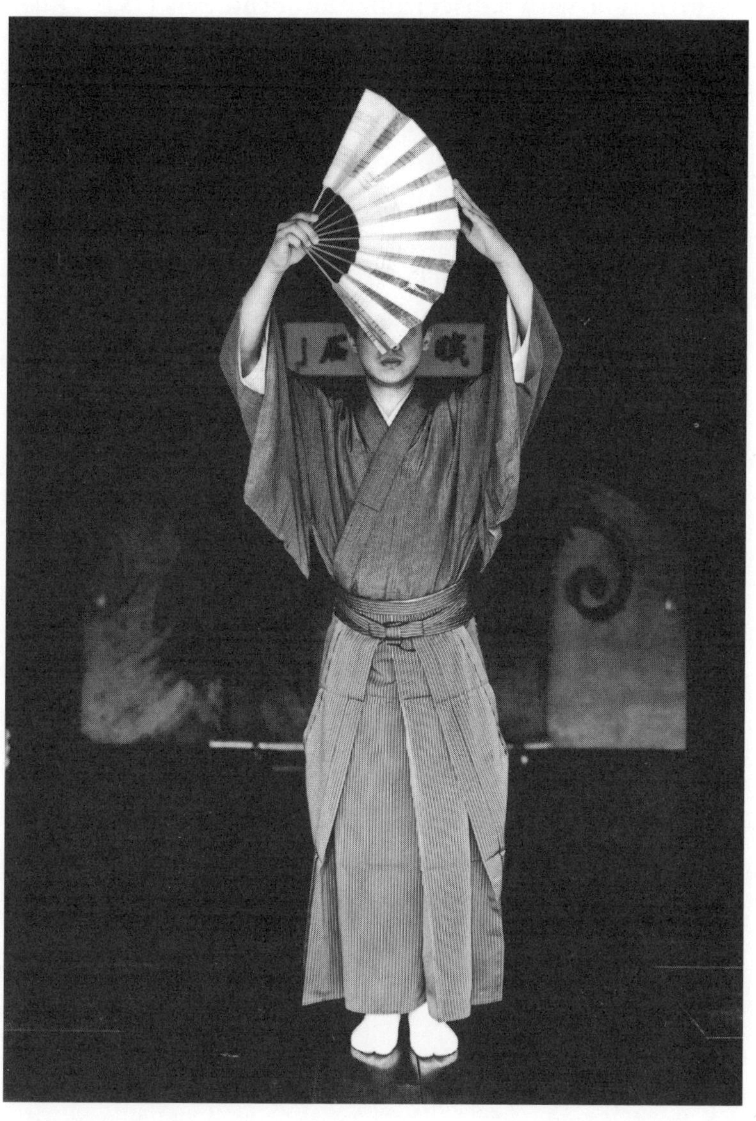

because of the delicate way he flexed his palm, from wrist to fingertips, with a discernment informed by his peculiar technique. Be that as it may, I was bewildered as to the source of the luster of his skin, which seemed to glow red from deep within. It was a completely ordinary Japanese hand, no different in color or luster from my own, lying on my lap. A second time and a third time, I compared my hand with that of Mr. Kongō, on the stage, but no matter how I scrutinized them, I could see no difference. The mystery was that the same hand, when seen on stage, came to seem bewitchingly beautiful while, on my lap, it seemed ordinary. This is the case not only with Mr. Kongō. In Noh, only very little of the actor's flesh shows beneath the costumes—no more than the face, the nape of the neck and the hands from wrists to fingertips, and in a role such as Yang Guifei, even the face is covered by a mask, and yet the color and luster of that flesh makes a strangely powerful impression. This is especially true of Mr. Kongō, but most actors' hands—ordinary, unremarkable Japanese hands— exert a fascination that goes unsuspected in contemporary clothes and make us open our eyes in wonder. I repeat, this is not limited to the most beautiful boys or handsome men of the stage. It would be absurd for us to be attracted by the lips of a man in our everyday life, but on the Noh stage their deep red tint and moist flesh possess a more fulsome sensuality than do a woman's vermilioned lips. Perhaps it is because the actor constantly wets his lips as he chants, but I cannot believe this is the only reason. Likewise, the blush of a child actor's face, that red tint, seems to stand out vividly on stage. In my experience, this is most noticeable against a costume in some shade of green; and while it is evident on the face of a pale child, that reddish blush looks even more striking on a dark face. That is because, on a pale child, the contrast between the white and red is too striking and slightly overpowers the dull, subdued colors of the Noh costume, while on a dark child's face, the red is less conspicuous, so that costume and face are each set off by a reciprocal glow. A subtle green and a subtle brown harmonize well, and the skin of the Yellow race looks its best against them, claiming our attention afresh. I don't know if such beauty, produced by a harmony of colors, is found anywhere else, but I believe that, if the Noh theater began to employ modern methods of stage lighting, as Kabuki has done, that aesthetic would be completely shattered. Therefore, we honor a necessary promise to maintain the Noh stage in its ancient darkness, and so the older the theater, the better. Floorboards that have acquired a natural polish, beams and panels that shine with a black luster, a stage shrouded in darkness above the actors' heads, from ridge pole to eaves, as deep as under a great temple bell— that is the ideal place for Noh, and in that sense, while it is certainly admirable that Noh is now performed in the Asahi Kaikan and various town halls, I fear that most of its distinctive character is lost in such a setting.[2]

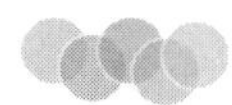

Incidentally, although the darkness that envelops Noh and the beauty it produces are a shadow world that today can be found only on the stage, it was not so very remote from everyday life in the past. That is because the darkness of the Noh stage was precisely the darkness of residential architecture of that time, and the patterns and colors of Noh costumes were approximately the same as those worn by most nobility and daimyo, if a bit showier. Once I let my mind wander this far, I imagine how much more beautiful than us today the Japanese of old must have been, especially those samurai who wore the extravagant apparel of the Sengoku or Momoyama period, and I fall into raptures at the mere thought. Noh certainly manifests the apex of male beauty in our countrymen; how gallant and dignified those ancient warriors must have looked on their way to and from ancient battlefields, their faces ruddy from the wind and rain, cheekbones bulging, figures clad in ceremonial dress of those somber colors and brilliant decoration, emblazoned with great family crests! I'm sure that, when people attend the Noh theater, each of them enjoys being immersed in such associations and, above and beyond the performance, they wax nostalgic thinking that the colorful world on the stage once existed in real life. Whereas the Kabuki stage is, on the contrary, a world of falsity in every respect, that bears no relation to the beauty of our reality. One cannot imagine seeing today, on that stage, the feminine beauty—or, needless to say, the masculine beauty—of old. Of course, in the Noh theater, those actors playing female roles wear masks, so it is altogether different from the real thing; nevertheless, no true feelings well up when watching an *onnagata* in a Kabuki play. This is entirely due to the excessive brightness of the Kabuki stage; possibly, back when there was no modern lighting equipment and the stage was barely illuminated by candles or oil lamps, the *onnagata* of the Kabuki stage were closer to real women. In any case, if people complain that the womanly *onnagata* of old are not to be found on the contemporary Kabuki stage, that is not necessarily the fault of the actors' skill or looks. If those *onnagata* of old were made to stand upon today's clearly lit stage, their harsh, manly contours that in the old days were concealed by a suitable gloom would doubtless be conspicuous. I saw Baikō perform O-Karu in his later years and felt this acutely.[3] I thought to myself: excessive illumination is destroying the beauty of Kabuki. A man about town in Osaka told me that the Bunraku puppet theater there had used lamps to illuminate the theater long after the Meiji era, and that it was much more suggestive. Even now, I sense more overpowering emotion from those puppets than from *onnagata* in Kabuki; if they were still lit by the dim glow of lamps, how gentle would the effect be—their characteristic stiffness erased, the gleam of their white faces shaded. It gives me chills just to imagine the beauty of the puppet theater in that age!

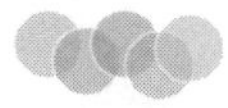

In Bunraku, the women puppets have only a face and hands. The puppeteer suggests movement sufficiently by manipulating the puppet with his hands inside the costume, which covers what would be the torso and legs. As far as I'm concerned, this is the closest thing on stage to reality, since women of old existed only above the collar and beyond the ends of their sleeves, everything else being altogether concealed by darkness. In those days, ladies of the middle class or above seldom left the home and, if they did, hid deep within some vehicle, so as not to display themselves on city streets. Mostly, though, they remained secluded on their property day and night, figures cloaked in darkness, existing only as a face. And while men's dress was relatively gaudy compared to today's, the same was not true of women's dress. The clothes worn by the wife or daughter of

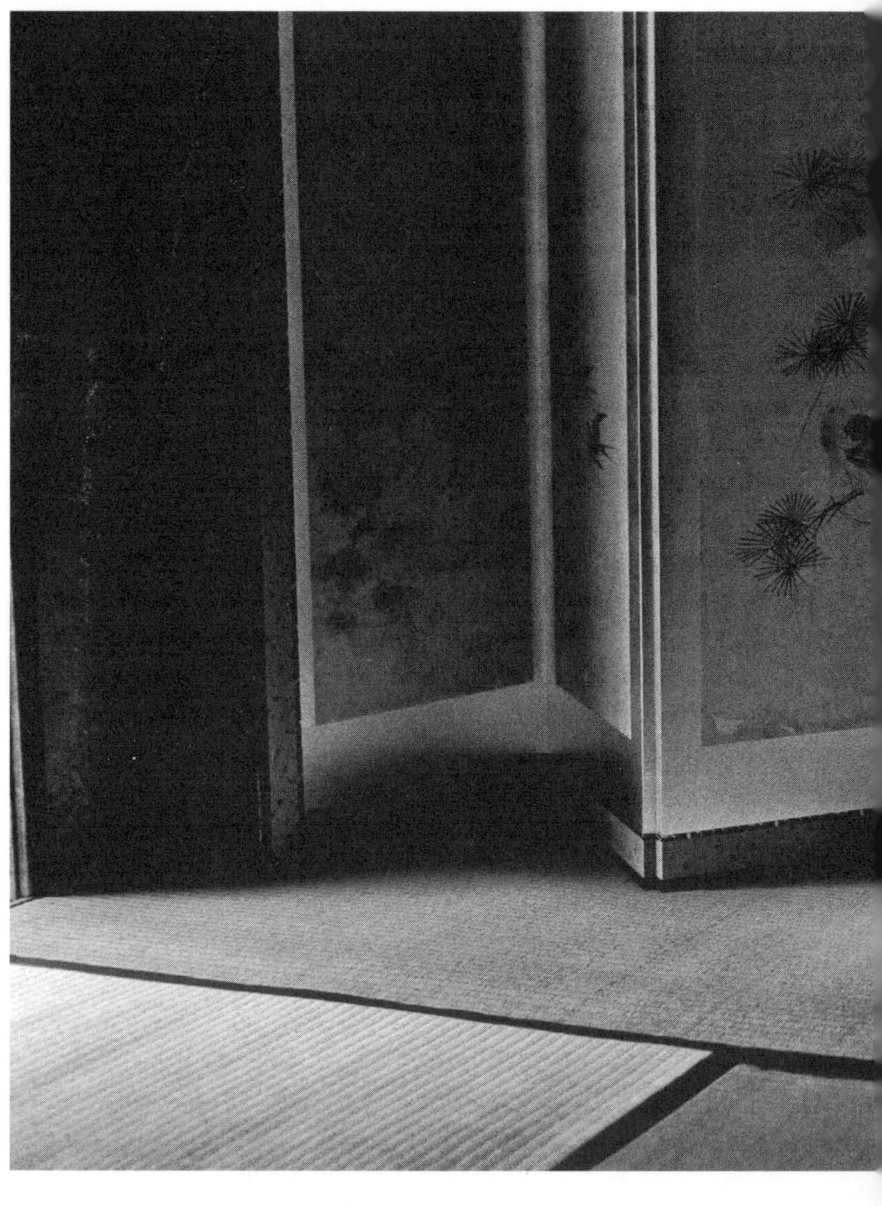

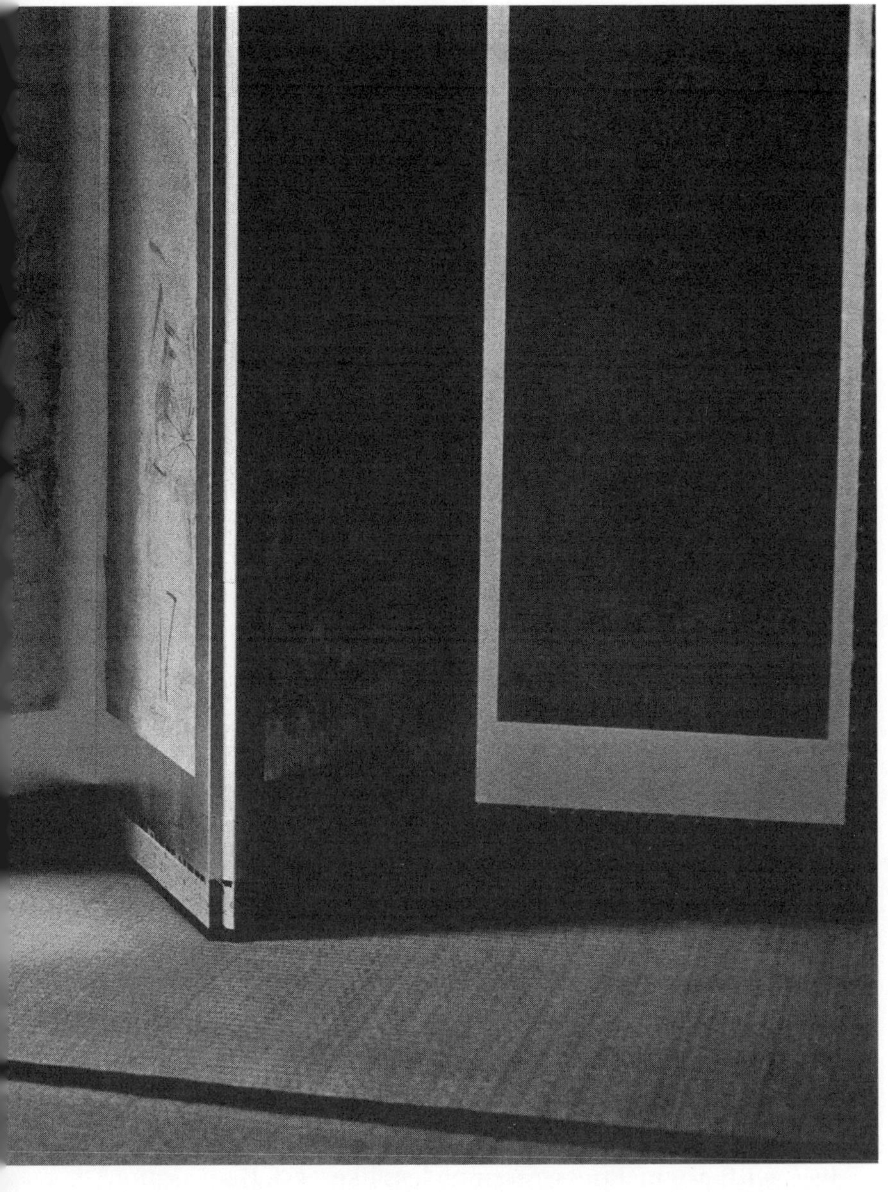

a merchant in the time of the shogunate were surprisingly sober. Their dress was one part of the overall darkness, part of the relationship between the darkness and their face. Such cosmetic practices as the blackening of teeth prevailed at that time, and if we consider the aim behind that, was it not to force even the mouth to bite down on the blackness, as if to cram every void—except the face— with the dark? Nowadays, this sort of feminine beauty can be found only in the rarified quarters of the Sumiya geisha house in Shimabara. And yet, if I think back to my child- hood and the face of my mother, doing needlework in the faint light of the courtyard at the back of our house in Ni- honbashi, I can imagine, just a bit, what the women of old were like. At that time (which is to say the Meiji twenties [1887–1896]), Tokyo merchant houses (*machiya*) were all dark, due to the architecture, and my mother, aunts and various other female relatives of a certain age, most of them, still blackened their teeth. As for their clothes, I can- not remember what they wore around the house, but, when going out, they usually dressed in a kimono with a small print on a gray ground. My mother was quite petite, not even five feet tall, as was usual for women then. Well, you might say those women had almost no flesh at all. Apart from her face and hands, I faintly remember my mother's legs, but I have little memory of her torso. The statue of Kannon in the Chūgū-ji temple reminds me of it; I suppose that is representative of the Japanese female body of an- tiquity.[4] The chest flat as a board, with paper-thin breasts, and even flatter belly, the straight line, without a single curve from back to waist to buttocks, the whole torso dis- proportionately withered, compared to the face, hands and feet, with no thickness, seeming less like flesh than a round rod—were not the bodies of women of that era, for the most part, of that sort? Even today one occasionally finds that sort of torso among elderly women of old-fashioned families, and among geisha. When I see them, I can't help thinking of the rods used to manipulate puppets. Truly, the torso of such a woman is just a rod to hang a costume from; nothing more. If you stripped off the layers of cotton batting and cloth, only a misshapen rod would remain— just like a puppet. But in the old days, that was enough. So long as they had their pale white face, those women living in the shadows had no need of a torso. I suppose, for those people who rejoice in the more physical beauty of the bright modern woman, it is difficult to imagine the ghostly beauty of those earlier ladies. For some, a beauty trumped up in murky light is not true beauty at all. However, as I stated above, we Easterners generate shadow from nothing and then create beauty from it. An ancient poem tells us, "What, gathered and tied, makes a brushwood hut, untied reverts to a field," and that quite accurately reflects our way of thinking: beauty inheres not in objects but in the pattern of shadow produced among them—in light and darkness. In short, our ancestors submerged women, as much as possible, in shade, just as they did lacquerware decorated with gold and silver inlay or mother-of-pearl, and wrapped their limbs in long sleeves and long hems, leaving only one spot, the nape of the neck, conspicuous. It's true that their bodies, poorly proportioned and lacking curves, might suffer in comparison to those of Western women, but there's no point thinking about what we cannot see. What we cannot see, we assume does not exist. Those who force themselves to see that ugliness drive away the beauty there, just as if they pointed a spotlight at the tokonoma.

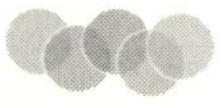

But why on earth is this tendency to seek beauty in the darkness pronounced only among peoples of the East? Westerners, too, spent ages without electricity, gas, or oil but, to my admittedly limited knowledge, they do not, by disposition, delight in shadows. Since ancient times, Japanese ghosts have had no feet; whereas Western ghosts have feet but are transparent. From even such a trivial example it is evident that *our* fantasies always contain jet-black darkness, while even their ghosts glimmer like glass. Likewise, all the crafts we use in daily life: for these, we prefer colors in which darkness has sedimented, while they prefer colors in which sunbeams are stacked up. Even silverware and copperware: we love the patina produced by tarnish, while they polish them until they sparkle, thinking tarnish dirty and unsanitary. They paint the walls and ceiling of their rooms white, so as not to create any dark corners. What produces this difference in tastes? I am afraid that we Easterners have a way of finding satisfaction in the circumstances we have been placed in and resign ourselves to our fate, and so we do not curse the darkness but endure it as something inevitable. If sunlight is scarce, we settle into the darkness and discover its particular beauty. Westerners, though, constantly seek a better situation. From candles to oil lamps, from lamps to gas lights, from gas lights to electric lights, they continually pursue brightness, striving to banish even the slightest shadow. I dare say a difference in temperament is one reason; however I would also like to consider whether it has to do with the difference in our skin color. We have prized pale skin above dark skin since ancient times and considered it more beautiful, yet the paleness of white people and our own paleness differ somehow. Individually, there are Japanese people paler than most Westerners and Westerners darker than most Japanese; however, if you look closely, the quality of the paleness and the darkness differs. I can speak from experience. I used to live in the Yamate neighborhood of Yokohama and went out, daytime and evening, with Westerners living in the foreign settlement there. I never thought their paleness was all that pale when I happened to see them as I amused myself in the reception rooms and dance halls they frequented. It was only when I saw them from a distance that I clearly understood the distinction between them and Japanese people. Among the Japanese were ladies dressed in evening gowns in no way inferior to the others', and with whiter skin than theirs, and yet, whenever one of them mixed with the Westerners I could immediately distinguish her from afar as Japanese. Which is to say, no matter how white a Japanese person may be, their whiteness is always slightly dusky. For this reason, those women, in order not to be defeated by their Western counterparts, heavily powder the exposed skin of their back, upper arms and armpits, and yet they cannot smother the dark shade at the base of their skin. You recognize it just as you recognize the bottom of a clear, blue lake when you survey it from a great height. Especially in the spaces between fingers, the area around the nostrils, the nape of the neck and the spine, dusky spots develop, as though dirt had collected there. Whereas with Westerners, even if the surface is cloudy, the base is bright and transparent, and dirty dark areas appear nowhere on their body. All is white and unblemished, from the top of their head to the tips of their toes. When one of us joins a gathering of them, it is like a spot of ink

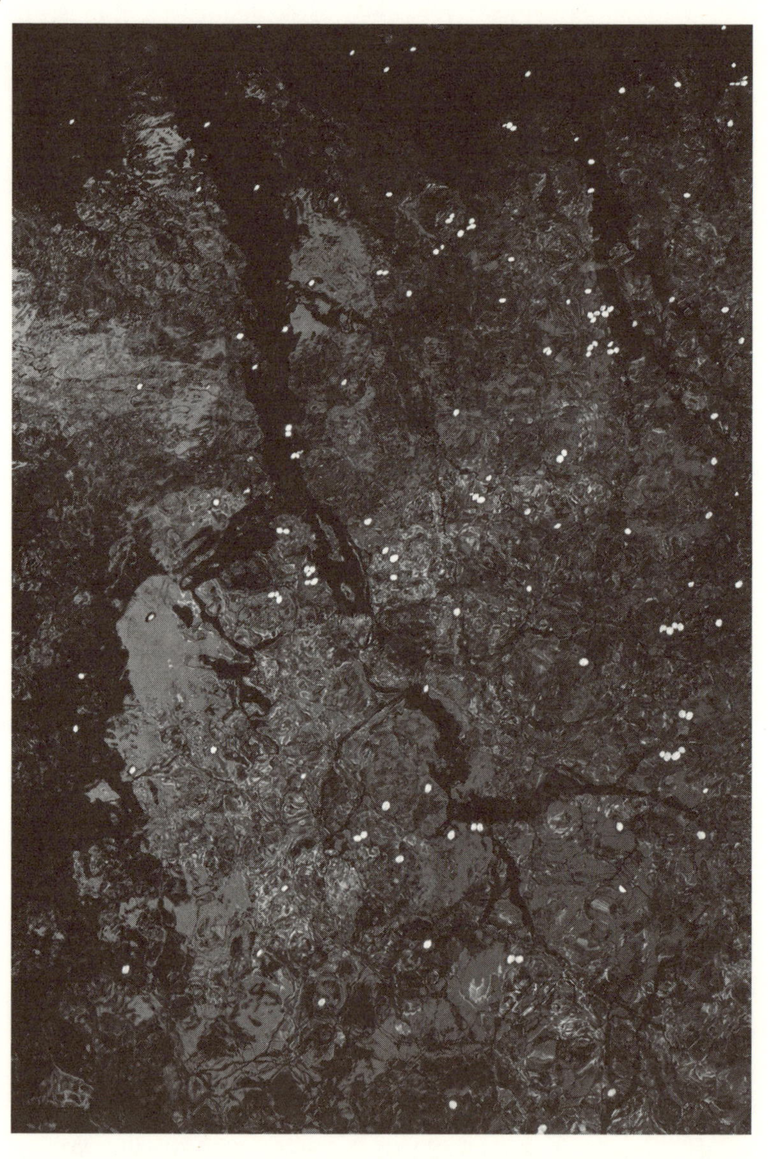

on a sheet of white paper, and even the rest of us find it uncomfortable to see, considering that person to be rather an eyesore. Looking at it this way, I can understand the mindset of fair-skinned peoples that rejected peoples of color.[5] Among white people, some especially high-strung types could not help but worry if the stain of even one or two people of color appeared at one of their social spaces. Come to that, I do not know how it is now but, at the time of the American Civil War, when the oppression of Black people was fiercest, white people's hatred and contempt was not reserved only for Black people but extended to children with one Black and one white parent, those whose parents were both of mixed race, those with one parent of mixed race and one white parent, and so on. They would not stop until they had investigated and persecuted the slightest trace of Black blood—one half, one quarter, one eighth, one sixteenth, one thirty-second. Even if someone were apparently indistinguishable from an unmixed white person, with blood only so mixed as to have one Black ancestor two or three generations back, their relentless eyes did not overlook even the very slightest pigmentation lurking beneath the pure white skin. When I think about such things, I understand how profoundly we of the yellow race are linked to this thing called "shadow." No one chooses to place himself in an unflattering situation, and so it is natural that we use dark colors for our food and the accoutrements of everyday life, submerging ourselves in a dark ambience. Even if our forefathers were not self-conscious of the fact that there was shade to their skin, even if they were unaware of the existence of a race whiter than themselves, I can only conclude that their sense for color naturally produced these tastes.

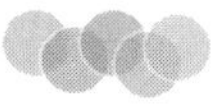

Our forefathers partitioned themselves off from the bright land, above and below and in all four directions, to make a world of shadow and, having sequestered their women in its darkest depths, convinced themselves that those women were the fairest in the world. This was inevitable and unobjectionable because whiteness of skin was the most indispensable condition of a woman's beauty. White people's hair is bright colored, while ours is dark; thus nature taught us the rules of darkness, which people of old unconsciously followed to make their yellow faces seem whiter. Above, I mentioned the practice of tooth-blackening; women of the past also used to shave their eyebrows, and was this, too, not also a technique to make the face conspicuous? And then, one thing I admire above all others is the blue lipstick that glitters like the shell of a beetle. It is hardly used anymore, except by the geisha of the Gion, and the allure of those lips can be understood only if one imagines it in flickering candlelight. The people of old intentionally painted a woman's red lips that bluish black color and coated them with powdered nacre. They drained the voluptuous face of any trace of blood. When I imagine a young woman in the dappled shade of a yew tree, occasionally parting her lips, blue as those of a will-of-the-whisp, to smile and let her lacquer-black teeth glitter—I cannot think of a whiter face than that. In the phantom world I describe in my mind, at least, she is even whiter than the white of any white woman. The white of white people is clear, obvious, ordinary, but hers is a kind of whiteness divorced from humanity. Or perhaps that whiteness doesn't really exist. Perhaps it is a fleeting trick of light and dark.

But that's fine. We do not wish for more. Here, as the obverse to the whiteness of such a face, I wish to speak of the color of the darkness that surrounds it. I have an unforgettable memory of seeing a certain darkness once, already several years ago, when I had the opportunity to introduce a guest of mine from Tokyo to the amusements at a geisha house in the Shimabara district, in Kyoto. There was a spacious salon called the Matsunoma that was later destroyed by fire, and the darkness of it, lit by one little candle, was different from the darkness of a smaller room. Just as we entered the room, a middle-aged hostess with shaved eyebrows and blackened teeth set a candle in front of a large screen and bowed. Behind the screen that defined a bright world of just a few square yards, a monochrome darkness sagged as though it had fallen from the ceiling, lofty and deep, and the uncertain light of the candle, unable to bore through that thickness, was repelled as though it had run into a black wall. Dear reader, have you ever seen this sort of "light-illumed darkness"? It is a substance somehow different from the darkness of a street at night. Each and every grain of it seemed filled with tiny, ash-like particles of a rainbow-colored radiance. I blinked reflexively, fearing they would get in my eyes. Today, it is generally fashionable to make such formal rooms smaller—only 6, 8, or 10 mats in area—and so one cannot see the color of the darkness there, even by candlelight. But high ceilings, wide corridors and reception room dozens of mats in size were usual in the palaces and brothels of old, and darkness always hung about their interiors like a fog. Then, high-born ladies-in-waiting were completely suspended in its scum. I wrote of this once, in *Ishōan zuihitsu* (Notes from Ishōan, 1932), but people today, having long since grown used to electric lighting, forget that there ever was such darkness.[6] The "visible darkness" of indoors seemed to possess some sort of flickering, shimmering quality, receptive to hallucination, so that, in some instances, it was more menacing than the darkness outdoors. Surely in such darkness occurred the pounce of a mountain demon or a changeling. And the women who lived within that darkness, heavily curtained and enclosed by layers of sliding screens—were they not, after all, the mountain demon's attendants? Darkness wrapped those womenfolk in tenfold, twentyfold layers, filling every gap: collars and cuffs and hems. No—perhaps, on the contrary, the darkness was vomited out from those women's bodies—from within their mouths with blackened teeth and from the tips of their black hair, like the Demon Spider, like its nest.

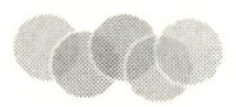

According to Takebayashi Musōan, who returned from Paris a few years ago, the nightscapes of Tokyo and Osaka are far brighter than those of European capitals.[7] While there are still houses lit only with gas lamps in Paris right on the Champs-Élysées, you cannot find even one such house in Japan unless you travel to some remote mountain village. I suppose America and Japan are the two nations in the world that use electric lighting most profligately; Japan is a country eager to imitate America in all things. Of course, Musōan was speaking of a time four or five years ago, when neon lights were not yet in widespread use; if he returned to Europe now, he would no doubt be surprised by how bright those cities have become. I was told by President Yamamoto of the journal *Kaizō* that once, when

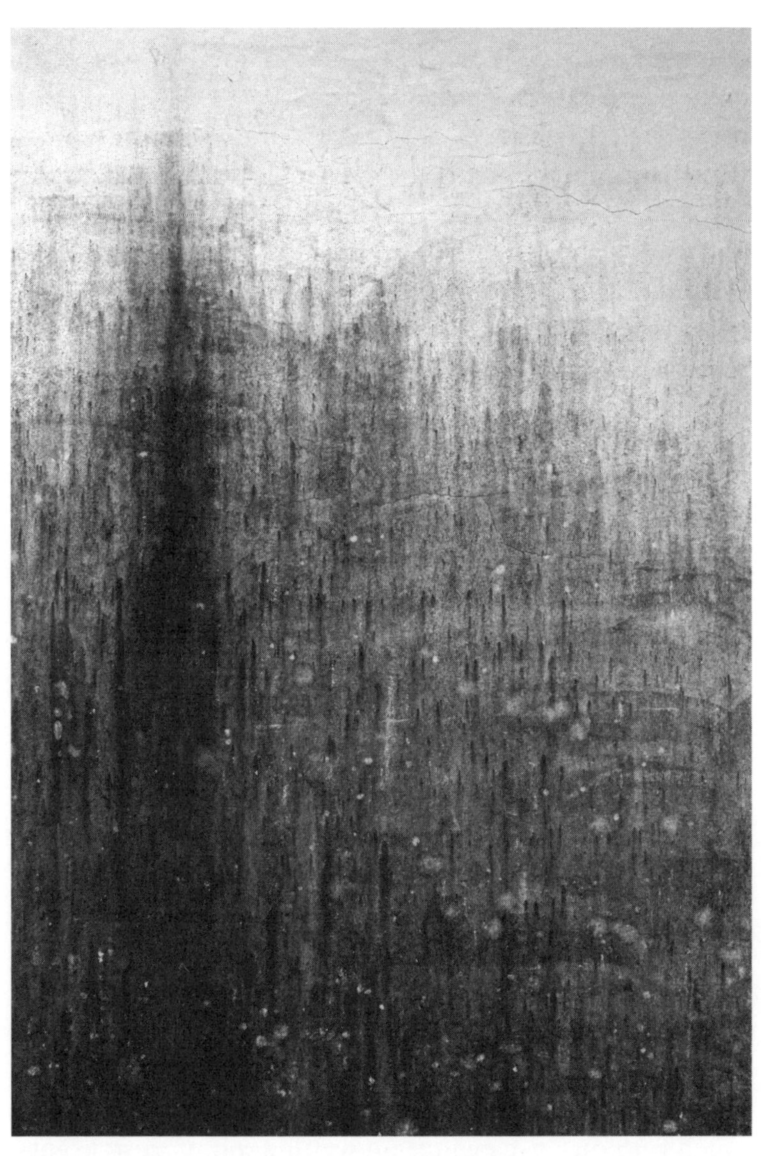

he was accompanying Albert Einstein on a tour of the Kamigata region, as their train passed Ishiyama, Einstein pointed out the window and said, "Ah, there is something quite wasteful," noting that the streetlights were lit in midday. Yamamoto added that Einstein was very attentive to that sort of thing, being Jewish.[8] At any rate, setting aside America, it is true that Japan uses electric lighting much more extravagantly than European nations do. Writing of Ishiyama reminds me of another odd occurrence. This past fall, after wracking my brains over the best place to hold a moon-viewing party, I decided on Ishiyama temple.[9] Then, the day before the full moon, I saw a newspaper article reporting that the temple had installed loudspeakers in the surrounding grove, over which they planned to broadcast the Moonlight Sonata to heighten the pleasure of those visiting. I immediately cancelled my plans. Not only do I detest loudspeakers, but I feared that, if the temple was installing them, it was probably also setting up illuminations here and there throughout the grounds and otherwise planning for a boisterous atmosphere. I also recall another, earlier instance when my plans for moon-viewing came to nothing. I had intended to take a boat out on the pond near Sumadera temple.[10] I got together a large party and ordered meals prepared in lacquer boxes, and so we set out for the pond, only to discover that the entire shoreline had been gaudily decorated with multicolored lights so bright you could hardly tell whether the moon was out or not. Such incidents suggest that we have recently become inured to electric lights and quite insensitive to the inconvenience of excessive illumination. It does not matter so much with moon-viewing, but waiting rooms, restaurants, inns, hotels and the like are far too wasteful with electric light. Although some degree of illumination is necessary to attract customers, when these places are lit up in the summer even before darkness falls, it's not only pointless but hot. Wherever I go in the summer, I am perplexed by this. If the indoors is ridiculously hot while the outdoors is cool, it is invariably because lightbulbs are too strong or too many. Turn off just a few lights and the room immediately cools down, but, inexplicably, neither the other customers nor the owners seem to recognize the problem. It is natural to keep a room brighter in the winter and darker in summer; fewer lights keep you cooler and, most important, attract fewer flying insects. But to turn on too many lights and then turn on a fan to cool the room down—it annoys me just to think of it. The heat dissipates quickly in a Japanese tatami room, so I can endure it there, but in Western-style rooms in hotels, not only is the ventilation poor, but the bedding, the ceiling, the floor and the four walls all absorb the heat and then release it back into the room, making it truly unbearable. Could anyone disagree with me who has, of a summer evening, visited the lobby of the Miyako Hotel in Kyoto (to cite one unfortunate example)? Situated as it is on a high plateau, the hotel boasts sweeping views of Mount Hiei and Mount Nyoigatake, the pagoda of Kurodani-san and the lush forests of Higashi-yama—the mere sight of which is refreshing. That is just why it is so regrettable. One sets out, on a summer evening, thinking to bask in the cooling sensation of mountain scenery and yearning for the breezes that fill the tower, only to find electric lights burning intensely within opal-glass globes that hang from that white ceiling. And because recent Western-style buildings have rather low ceilings, it feels as though balls of fire are spinning just over one's head; it could not feel any hotter. And the lower the ceiling, the hotter one's body—as if one were being broiled, from head, to neck, to spine. Furthermore, even though just one of those balls of fire would light the space sufficiently, there are three or four glowing from the ceiling and I don't know how many smaller lights running along the walls and the pillars besides—so many that I cannot imagine what purpose they serve except to eliminate the slightest darkness from every corner. As a result, there is no shade at all inside, and the combination of white walls, thick red pillars and gaudily colored, mosaic-like carpet saturates the eye like a freshly printed lithograph, and this, too, contributes to a hot and stuffy sensation. As you step into such a room from the corridor, you notice a significant rise in the temperature. Even if cool night air flows in, it quickly becomes a hot breeze, and so serves no purpose. I used to stay at that hotel from time to time, and so these criticisms are kindly meant, and offered out of nostalgia, but it is a shame that such an ideal place to enjoy the scenic vistas and the cool air in summer has been utterly ruined by electric lighting. Never mind Japanese people; Westerners, too, must find such heat unbearable, no matter how much they appreciate the brightness. They would comprehend it immediately if they just once tried turning down the lights. This is only one example, however; the problem is by no means limited to that hotel. The Imperial Hotel is still bearable, since it uses indirect lighting, but I think they, too, would do better to keep the rooms darker in the summer. At any rate, the illumination of today's interiors is no longer a matter of providing light for reading, or writing, or sewing; rather, it is used to eliminate shade entirely from the room, but this attitude is, at the very least, incompatible with the beauty of the Japanese home. People minimize their use of electricity at home for reasons of economy, so that's fine, but when a house is part of the hospitality business, the halls, the stairwell, the entrance, the garden, the front gate—it all eventually becomes over-illuminated, so that the floors, as well as the garden ponds and stones, lose all depth. It is warmer in winter, and that is of some benefit, but in the summer, no matter to what secluded spot you flee from the heat, if you are headed to an inn, you are generally bound to meet with the same grief as at the Miyako Hotel. I have therefore determined that the best way to draw the cool air is to throw open the storm shutters on the four sides of my own home, hang mosquito netting in the pitch-black interior, and lie down within it.

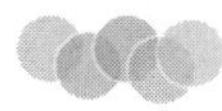

I recently read an article in some journal or newspaper in which elderly Englishwomen were lamenting the difference between young people of the past and today. They complained that, in their own youth, they had esteemed their elders and cared for them, whereas young people today demonstrate no such regard but consider the elderly filthy and avoid them. I was struck that elderly people of no matter what country say the same thing and that, as people age, they come to think the past better in every respect. The elderly of a century ago yearned for the era two centuries earlier, and the elderly of two centuries ago yearned for the era three centuries earlier, so that no age is ever satisfied with its present conditions. Above and beyond the recent rapid progress of culture generally, there are the special circumstances of our country, which has

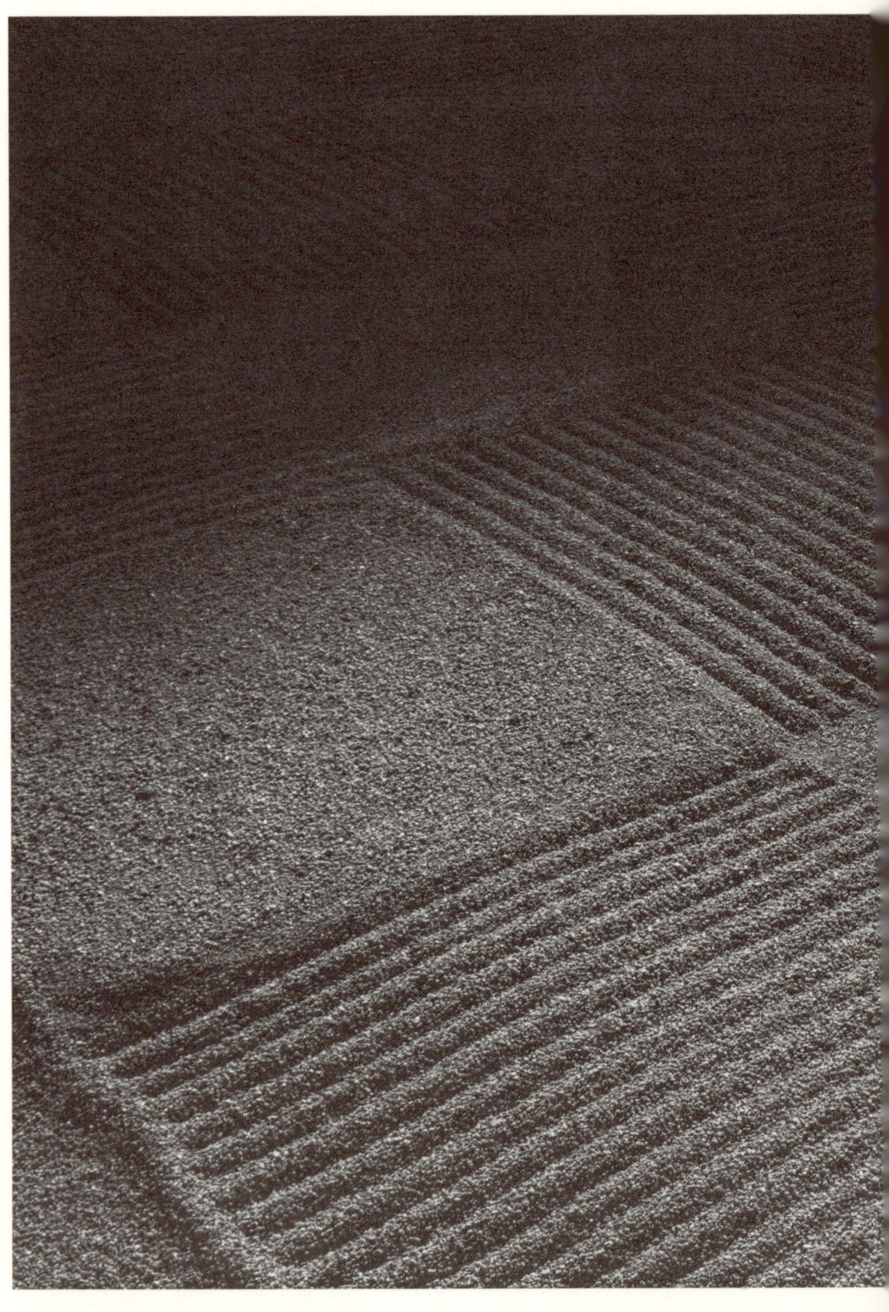

weathered as much change in the decades since the Meiji Restoration as we did in the preceding three or four centuries. It is strange for me to say such things, mouthing the words of the elderly as though I had become some senior figure myself; however I do feel that the conveniences of the modern age are entirely geared to the young, and make this an increasingly inhospitable era for anyone older. To put it plainly, when we must wait for a signal before crossing an intersection, then it is no longer safe for senior citizens to walk around town. It is fine for fancy people who ride about in cars, but I tremble all over when I try to cross a street on an occasional trip into Osaka. Even if there is a traffic light on the side of the road, it can be difficult to tell whether the green or the red light is blinking (though the ones that stand in the middle of the road are visible enough), and at a big intersection, I sometimes get the various lights confused. When Kyoto installed officers in intersections to direct the traffic, I really thought, Well, that's the limit. Now, if you want to savor the atmosphere of a traditional Japanese town, you must go to Nishinomiya, Sakai, Wakayama, Fukuyama, or another such smaller city. When it comes to food, too, you must search long and hard to find anything in the great metropolises that suits the more mature palate. Just the other day a newspaper columnist visited and asked me to talk about some unusual delicacies, so I explained the method by which people up in the remote area around Mount Yoshino, in Nara, make *kakinohazushi*—sushi wrapped in persimmon leaves. While I'm at it, I might as well write it down here. First, cook rice, adding one *gō* (180 milliliters) of sake to each *shō* (1.8 liters) of rice. Add the sake just as the rice and water start to boil. When the rice is done, let it cool completely and then, with your hands salted, press it into balls. Your hands must not be wet at all; the key is to press the rice balls using only salt. Then thinly slice a salted salmon, lay a piece on top of each rice ball, and wrap that in a persimmon leaf, the top of the leaf facing in, having blotted both the salmon and the leaf with a dry dishcloth in advance. Then, take a sushi mold or wooden rice tub, perfectly dry, and pack the rice balls into it, from edge to edge, leaving no gaps; cover with a lid; and place a stone on top, of the sort used for pickling. If you prepare them in the evening, you can eat them from the next day, but the flavor improves over time, and they are good for two or three days. You use a knotweed leaf to sprinkle vinegar over the sushi before eating. A friend who visited Yoshino found this dish so delicious that he learned how to make it and then taught me, and though it is a local specialty, it can be made anywhere, so long as you have a persimmon tree and a salted salmon. If you try it at home, you will find that it really is delicious—just remember to eliminate all excess moisture and cool the cooked rice completely. The way the oil from the salmon and the salt soak into the rice and season it, and, on the other hand the salmon softens as though it were fresh, is indescribable. The flavor is quite distinct from Tokyo-style *nigiri* sushi, and I prefer it. I practically lived on it this past summer. In any case, I was impressed by the ingenuity of those mountain people, so poor in resources, to have come up with this way of eating salted salmon. But then, by inquiring into various local foodways, one discovers that country folk have much more reliable palates than city folk these days and enjoy luxuries we cannot imagine. And so, the elderly give up on the city, little by little, and seek a secluded life in the countryside. But then the rural town installs fancy streetlights and so on, year by year becoming just like Kyoto, so one can never settle down. It is said that, before long, enlightenment will take another step forward and new modes of transportation will extend into the sky and underground so that the street level will grow quiet again, as it was in an earlier age, but it seems certain that, even if such an age arrives, it will bring new inventions to torment the elderly. Keep out of the way, they are told, and so eventually there is no place left for them except cowering in their homes, enjoying some homemade snack with their evening drink, perhaps listening to the radio. If you think only the elderly voice such complaints, you are mistaken. Recently, the author of the "Tensei jingo" column in the *Osaka Asahi* newspaper berated Osaka prefectural officials for ordering, without authority, that wooded areas be cleared for the construction of an access road to Minō Park, and the mountain forest thinned; I was shocked to read it.[11] Dispossessing us of even the shadows under trees in the deepest forest—that truly is the most heartless sort of work. At this rate, every famous spot in Nara and the suburbs of Kyoto and Osaka will gradually be reduced to a bald hilltop as the cost of its popularity. But this is just another variety of complaint, while in fact I do feel profound gratitude for the spirit of the current age. At this point, no matter what I might say, Japan is already committed to following the path of Western culture, and there is no choice but to push forward, leaving the elderly behind. However, so long as we cannot change the color of our skin, we must resolve to walk that path carrying on our backs, for all eternity, a burden imposed upon us alone. This, finally, is the meaning of what I have written: I wonder whether there is no path left to us somewhere—perhaps in literature or the

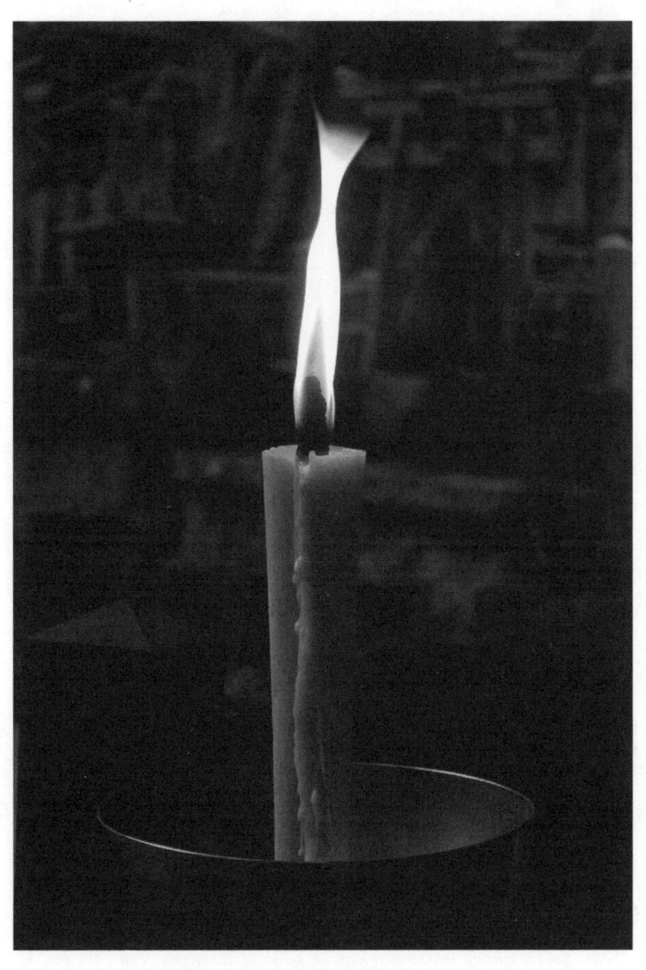

fine arts—to compensate for this indemnity. I want to summon once more, if only within the domain of literature, our world of shadow that is now disappearing. I want to extend the eaves of that sanctuary called literature, darken its walls, push back into the shadows those things that have been over-exposed, and strip away useless decoration. It need not be done to every house—just one will do. To discover what it would it be like, we must first try turning out the lights.

Endnotes

1. *Kōtei* was written by Kanze (Kojirō) Nobumitsu (1435 or 1450–1516), one of the great playwrights of Noh's golden age. Kongō Iwao (1886–1951) was the twenty-fourth generational head of the Kongō line of Noh actors. Yang Guifei (719–756) is a historical figure, consort of the Tang emperor Xuanzong and one of the celebrated Four Beauties of ancient China.

2. The parent company of the *Osaka Asahi Shinbun* newspaper opened the Asahi Kaikan in 1926. It hosted concerts, theater performances, art exhibitions and other events until closing in 1962.

3. Presumably the sixth of this line, Onoe Baikō VI (1870–1934), who held this name from 1903 until his death.

4. Chūgū-ji is a temple in Nara, founded by Shōtoku Taishi in the seventh century. The main hall holds a statue of Nyoirin Kannon, carved from camphor wood and dating to the Asuka period (538–710). The statue is a National Treasure.

5. Tanizaki is drawing a contrast between two groups. The first group he calls *hakuseki jinshu*, *jinshu* meaning a "race," an "ethnos," or a "people." I have translated *hakuseki* as "fair-skinned" to distinguish this group from *hakujin*, a more common term Tanizaki uses elsewhere (including the very next clause) to signify "white person/people." The second group he calls *yūshoku jinshu*, *yūshoku* conveying the sense expressed today by the term "of-color."

6. "Ishōan," or "hermitage of the leaning pine," is the name Tanizaki gave to his home in the Sumiyoshi neighborhood of Kobe.

7. Takebayashi Musōan (1880–1962) was a novelist. See also p. 70.

8. Yamamoto Sanehiko (1885–1952) founded the publishing company Kaizōsha and began publishing the general-interest journal *Kaizō* (Reconstruction) in 1919. In 1922, the company invited Albert Einstein to Japan to give a series of lectures. Tanizaki's novel *Manji* (*Quicksand*) was first serialized in *Kaizō* between 1928 and 1930. The journal ceased publication in 1955.

9. The moon-viewing festival celebrates the harvest moon, taking place on the fifteenth night of the eighth moon of the lunar cycle.

10. Sumadera, in Kobe, was established in 886. The titular protagonist of the *Tale of Genji* makes the temple his home in exile.
11. This column, which still appears on the front page of the *Asahi Shimbun*, debuted in the *Osaka Asahi* in 1904. The name refers to the Latin expression "*vox populi, vox dei*," that is, "the voice of the people is the voice of God."

First published by Tuttle Publishing, an imprint of Periplus Editions (HK) Ltd.

www.tuttlepublishing.com

English translation © 2025 Michael P. Cronin
Photographs © 2025 John Einarsen
Cover photo: Komyo-in temple, Kyoto, by John Einarsen

Library of Congress Catalog-in-Publication Data in progress

ISBN: 978-4-8053-1935-2

29 28 27 26   5 4 3 2 1   2601VP

Printed in Malaysia

GPSR Representative
Matt Parsons, matt.parsons@upi2mbooks.hr
UPI-2M PLUS d.o.o., Medulićeva 20, 10000 Zagreb, Croatia

Distributed by:

North America, Latin America & Europe
Tuttle Publishing
364 Innovation Drive
North Clarendon
VT 05759 9436, USA
Tel: 1(802) 773 8930
Fax: 1(802) 773 6993
info@tuttlepublishing.com
www.tuttlepublishing.com

Asia Pacific
Berkeley Books Pte Ltd
3 Kallang Sector #04-01
Singapore 349278
Tel: (65) 6741-2178
Fax: (65) 6741-2179
inquiries@periplus.com.sg
www.tuttlepublishing.com

Japan
Tuttle Publishing
Yaekari Building, 3rd Floor
5-4-12 Osaki Shinagawa-ku
Tokyo 141 0032 Japan
Tel: 81 (3) 5437 0171
Fax: 81 (3) 5437 0755
sales@tuttle.co.jp
www.tuttle.co.jp

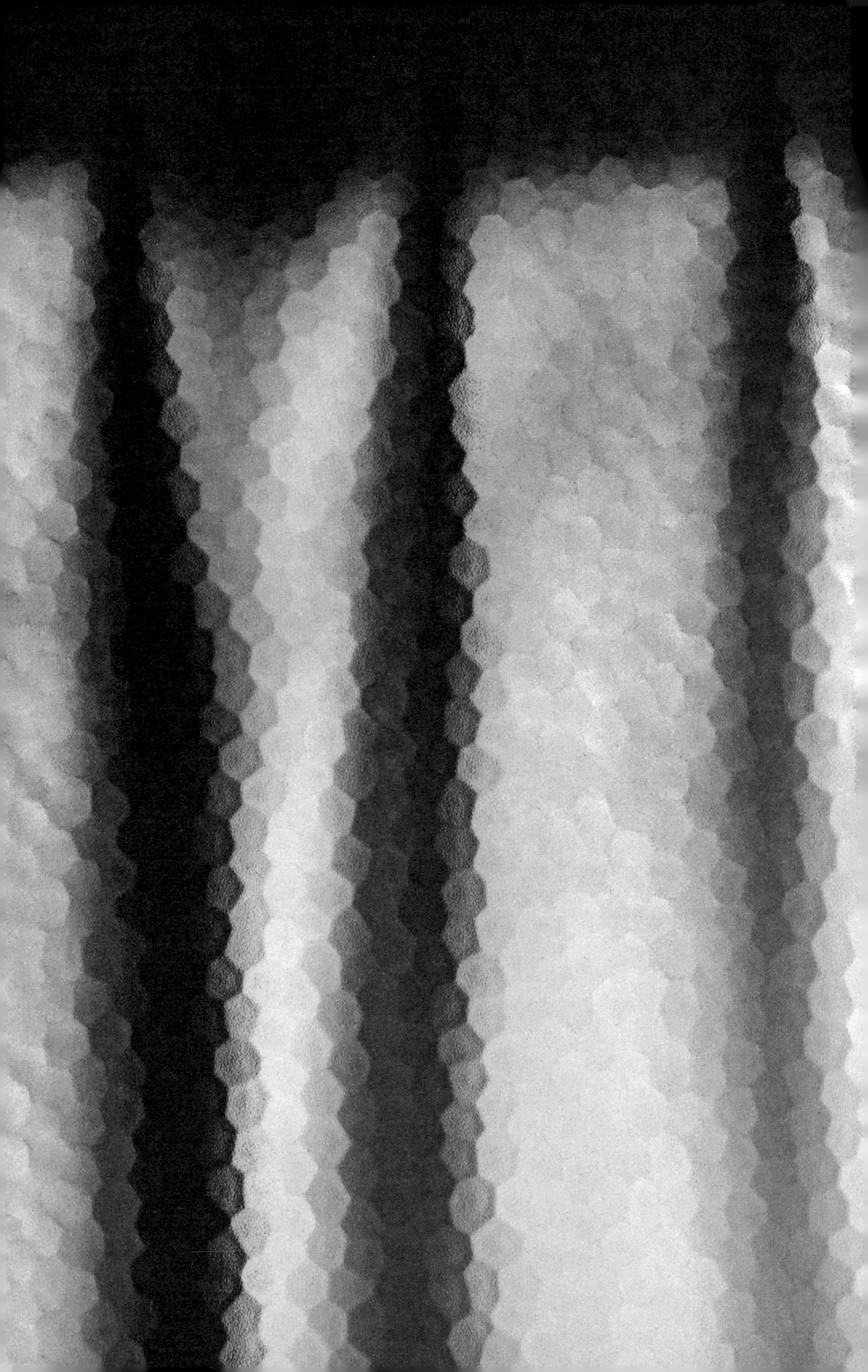